Religion Revision for Junior Certificate
Second Edition

Niall and Anne Boyle

Gill & Macmillan

Gill & Macmillan Ltd
Hume Avenue
Park West
Dublin 12
with associated companies throughout the world
www.gillmacmillan.ie

© Niall and Anne Boyle 2006, 2007
© Artwork by Karen Allsop and Design Image
978 07171 4132 6
Print origination in Ireland by TypeIT, Dublin

The paper used in this book is made from the wood pulp of managed forests. For every tree felled, at least one tree is planted, thereby renewing natural resources.

All rights reserved.

No part of this publication may be copied, reproduced or transmitted in any form or by any means without written permission of the publishers or else under the terms of any licence permitting limited copying issued by the Irish Copyright Licensing Agency.

Contents

Introduction	1
Section A	
Chapter 1 Communities of Faith	9
Section B Foundations of Religion	
Chapter 2 Christianity	27
Section C Foundations of Religion	
Chapter 3 Judaism	57
Chapter 4 Islam	66
Chapter 5 Buddhism	71
Section D	
Chapter 6 The Question of Faith	79
Section E	
Chapter 7 The Celebration of Faith	93
Section F	
Chapter 8 The Moral Challenge	121
Glossary	133
Exam Papers	139

Introduction

The aims of Junior Cycle Religious Education are:

- to provide students with a framework for encountering and engaging with the variety of religious traditions in Ireland and elsewhere
- to promote an understanding and appreciation of why people believe, as well as tolerance and respect for the values and beliefs of all
- to prepare students for the responsibilities of citizenship.

Source: *Department of Education*

SYLLABUS

Students can choose to take Junior Certificate Religious Education at either Higher Level or Ordinary Level. The *syllabus* (course to be studied) is divided into two parts.

Part One

Students must study any *two* of the following:
Section A: Communities of Faith
Section B: Foundations of Religion – Christianity
Section C: Foundations of Religion — Major World Religions (choose one from Hinduism, Judaism, Buddhism and Islam).

Part Two

Students must study *all three* of the following:
Section D: The Question of Faith
Section E: The Celebration of Faith
Section F: The Moral Challenge.

ASSESSMENT

The assessment of Junior Certificate Religious Education has two elements:
1 a final two-hour written examination
2 a pre-submitted journal work booklet.

Marks

Total marks that can be awarded = 500 marks.
The exam paper is worth 80 per cent of the total = 400 marks.
The journal work is worth 20 per cent of the total = 100 marks.

Examination Paper

(based on 2004 example)

TABLE I.1 Higher Level

Section No.	Question Type	Marks Available	Time Allowed	No. of Questions	Must Answer
1	One-line/tick the box	50	15 min	20	Any 10
2	Visual-based	30	15 min	4	Any 3
3	Article-based	50	15 min	4	All
4	Detailed analysis	200	55 min	6	Any 4
5	Short essay	70	20 min	6	Any 1

Total marks for paper = 400

INTRODUCTION

TABLE I.2 Ordinary Level

Section No.	Question Type	Marks Available	Time Allowed	No. of Questions	Must Answer
1	One-line/ tick the box	80	20 min	20	Any 10
2	Visual-based	60	20 min	4	Any 3
3	Article-based	60	20 min	3	All
4	Detailed analysis	200	60 min	6	Any 5

Total marks for paper = 400

Journal Work

Both Higher Level *and* Ordinary Level students must complete the Journal Work component of the Junior Certificate Religious Education programme. They must choose *one* topic from a list of approved titles that is issued to schools. Then they must submit their finished work in a special booklet provided for them by the State Examinations Commission.

General Guidelines for Completion of the Journal Booklet
Titles for journal work are the same for Ordinary Level and Higher Level.
   Students are requested to submit journal work on *one* title only.
   In undertaking journal work students may work in groups or undertake a visit or investigation as a whole class. However, each student must complete and submit an individual journal for assessment. The cues/prompts in each section of the booklet may be used where relevant to assist students in completing their journals.
   Students may draw diagrams/illustrations in the Journal Booklet. They should not, however, attach or affix material to the Journal Booklet.

1. Introduction
In completing the Journal Booklet Section One the student should:
- indicate whether he/she did journal work on his/her own, or as part of a group/whole class

- identify the title he/she chose from the prescribed list for journal work
- give a personal title to their journal work that is relevant to the prescribed title and indicative of the student's own personal experience
- state the reason why he/she personally chose this title. (Explain how the chosen title generated personal interest or enthusiasm, or why he/she had a particular concern about this topic)
- describe what he/she hoped to achieve/learn/find out by doing journal work on the chosen title.

2. Getting started
In completing the Journal Booklet Section Two the student should:

- describe the way(s) he/she planned to personally engage with the chosen title and identify the skill(s) he/she hoped to use.

3. Work
In completing the Journal Booklet Section Three the student should:

- describe the work in which he/she personally engaged. (If the student did journal work as part of a group/whole class, he/she should describe the work in which the group or whole class engaged, as well as the work done by him/her personally)
- state the reason why he/she chose this way of doing journal work
- describe his/her reaction to the work engaged in for the journal. (If the student did journal work as part of a group/whole class, he/she should describe the reaction of the group or whole class, as well as indicating whether it was similar to or different from his/her own personal reaction.)

4. Discoveries
In completing the Journal Booklet Section Four the student should:

- state what he/she learned from doing journal work on the chosen title
- describe the effect doing journal work had on him/her
- identify two skills he/she used in doing journal work on this title and describe how he/she used them
- identify two links between his/her journal work and other aspects of the Junior Certificate Religious Education course.

INTRODUCTION

5. Looking Back
In completing the Journal Booklet Section Five the student should:

- reflect on and evaluate how he/she approached doing journal work on his/her chosen title
- indicate what went well in his/her journal work
- identify how he/she would do journal work differently if starting again.

Source: *Department of Education*

The finished booklet is submitted for external assessment along with the examination paper.

> *Concerning Dates*
> B.C. = Before Christ
> A.D. = Anno Domini (a Latin phrase meaning 'In the year of Our Lord')
>
> Alternatively, the abbreviations B.C.E. (Before the Common Era) may be used instead of B.C. and C.E. (Common Era) may be used instead of A.D.

Section A

1 Communities of Faith

COMMUNITY

Meaning

Human beings are *social* creatures. We need to have the friendship and support of others. We need to belong. We need to live in *community*.

Community exists wherever people

- live and work together
- share similar interests
- hold broadly similar views about life.

Examples
We can consider community under the following headings:

1 Local
   - family/friends
   - residents' association
   - sports club.

2 National
   - political party
   - charitable organisation, e.g. Society of St Vincent de Paul
   - trade union.

3 International
   - Friends of the Earth
   - Red Cross
   - United Nations Organisation.

Importance

Human beings have different *needs*. For example:

- *physical needs*: food, water, clothing and shelter
- *emotional needs*: to be loved and respected for oneself
- *security needs*: a stable, orderly and safe place in which to live/learn/work.

A community should help people to fulfil their different needs. Sometimes, however, communities can fail to do so. Consider how:

- some people (e.g. homeless people) can have their needs ignored and be *isolated*
- some people (e.g. refugees) can be deliberately made to feel unwelcome and be *rejected*.

Other people, however, are not content to let this happen. They join organisations that try to help those whose needs are not being met.

COMMUNITIES AT WORK

The Simon Community

- Homelessness is a growing problem in Ireland. The Simon Community assists over 3,000 homeless people each year.
- The Simon Community was founded in England in 1963 by Anton Wallich-Clifford.
- He was inspired by the work of other social reformers such as Dorothy Day (USA) and Mario Borrelli (Italy).
- He wanted to create houses of hospitality in which both the homeless and the housed lived in community.
- In time, he established a network of care centres based on the principle of accepting people as they are and offering them practical assistance, i.e. food and accommodation.
- The Simon Community opened its first Irish centre in Dublin in 1969. Others were later set up in Cork, Dundalk and Galway. Together these form the national federation called the Simon Community of Ireland.

- These centres offer care for the homeless (e.g. soup runs, a safe place to sleep) and try to challenge Irish society to tackle the root causes of homelessness.
- People can help the Simon Community by: volunteering to work with the homeless; raising funds to support its work; writing to their local TDs to ask for more affordable housing to be made available.

The Samaritans

- The Samaritans were founded by Rev. Chad Varah, Rector of St Stephen's Anglican Church, London, in 1953.
- He discovered that people who were considering suicide (i.e. taking their own lives) often found being befriended by ordinary people more acceptable and effective than professional counselling.
- The befriending service offered by the Samaritans is available 24 hours a day, every day of the year.
- All Samaritans obey the same strict rules:
  1. they guarantee complete secrecy about the identity of callers
  2. the caller (either by telephone or in person) will never be contacted by the Samaritans unless he/she specifically requests it
  3. they have no 'message' except that there is someone ready to listen and befriend a person in need, day or night.
- All Samaritans are volunteers. They come from all walks of life. Usually only members of their immediate family know that they are Samaritans. They are known to callers only by their first name.
- The Samaritans offer callers time, treat them with respect and take what they say seriously. There is no problem that they will refuse to discuss.

COMMUNITIES OF FAITH

Meaning

A community of faith exists wherever people have a *religion* in common. Religion involves *belief in and worship of a god or gods*.

Different Types of Religion

- *Monotheism*: the belief that there is only *one* God.
- *Polytheism*: the belief that there are *many* gods.
- *Henotheism*: when a person believes in one god but does not deny the existence of other gods.

MAJOR WORLD RELIGIONS

There are five major world religions.

TABLE 1.1

Religion	Founder(s)	Date
Hinduism	Unknown holy men	c. 2000 B.C.
Judaism	Abraham Moses	c. 1850 B.C. c. 1300 B.C.
Buddhism	Siddhartha Gautama	c. 500 B.C.
Christianity	Jesus Christ	c. 6–4 B.C.
Islam	Muhammad	A.D. 622

Common Characteristics

While there are many differences between the major world religions, they all share certain characteristics.

1 Creed
A set of beliefs that is shared by all the members of a religion.
Example: the *Shahadah* in Islam – *There is no God but Allah, and Muhammad is his prophet.*

2 Sacred Text
A holy book containing the important stories and key teachings of a religion.

COMMUNITIES OF FAITH

TABLE 1.2

Religion	Sacred text
Hinduism	The Vedas
Judaism	The Tenakh
Buddhism	The Pali Canon
Christianity	The Bible
Islam	The Qur'an

3 Code
A set of guidelines that help people to decide whether an action is right or wrong.

Example: the *Ten Commandments*.

4 Ritual
Religious ceremonies that give a regular pattern to people's worship of God.
Example: A ritual of initiation such as the *rite of circumcision* for Jewish males.

5 Symbol
Rituals celebrate the invisible presence of God. Religions use symbols to make God *visible* and *accessible* to people.

A symbol is a concrete image, word or gesture that points beyond itself, but has more than one meaning.

Example: the use of *oil, water* and *candles* in the Christian sacrament of baptism.

6 Calendar
This marks the passage of time and indicates the holy days of a particular religion, when special rituals are held to remember important moments in its history.

Example: *Christmas Day,* when Christians celebrate the birth of Jesus.

COMMUNITIES OF FAITH AT WORK

Giving Witness in Christianity

All the Christian churches teach that their members are called to *give witness* to their faith in Jesus Christ. This means they must demonstrate their love for God by the way they live.

Each person has a unique *vocation* (i.e. calling) to serve God by helping other people.

Many Christians seek to do so through their commitment to:

- family life
- work
- voluntary organisations.

Some Christians believe that their vocation is to commit themselves full-time to do certain work as members of a religious community.

Religious Communities

In the Catholic and Orthodox Churches, a person may enter religious life:

- if a man, as a *monk* in a monastery
- if a woman, as a *nun* in a convent.

Each monk or nun belongs to a specific religious order. These religious orders can be grouped under two headings.

Apostolic Communities
These undertake specific work in the community, such as caring for the poor, the sick and the homeless.

Contemplative Communities
These communities live enclosed lives. Their members rarely, if ever, leave their monastery or convent and they devote all their time to prayer, study and physical work.

After completing their training, all monks/nuns must take the same basic *vows* (solemn promises). These are:

- *poverty:* not to be tied down by worldly possessions but to share their goods
- *chastity:* to refrain from sexual relationships and devote all their energies to prayer and good works
- *obedience:* to be completely dedicated to God and work for the good of the community.

All monks/nuns live according to a *rule* (i.e. a detailed code of conduct). Important Catholic religious orders include:

- the Dominicans (education of young people)
- the Sisters of Charity (care of the disabled)
- the Order of St John of God (care of the sick).

RELATIONSHIPS BETWEEN COMMUNITIES OF FAITH

Inter-faith Dialogue

Inter-faith dialogue involves the *members of the different world religions talking with and listening to one another.*

Inter-faith dialogue is rooted in the idea of *pluralism,* i.e. there is plenty of room on earth for everyone and people of different religions should learn to live alongside one another in peace.

The purposes of inter-faith dialogue are:

- to achieve *mutual understanding,* i.e. to gain a clear idea of what each other believes
- to combat prejudice and foster *mutual respect* for and *tolerance* of each other's different views
- to work together in matters of *common interest,* e.g. combating injustice
- to *prevent conflict* between people of different religions.

All this does not mean that any of the major world religions believes that one religion is just as good as another. Each of these religions still strongly asserts that it alone offers the best and most complete set of answers to the mysteries of life. However, they do admit that each can learn from one another and work together to make the world a better place.

Christianity: Three Traditions

All Christians claim to be followers of Jesus Christ. However, over the centuries Christians have become divided into different groups: Catholic, Orthodox and Protestant.

One way of seeing this is to think of the Christian religion as a great tree. The roots of the tree are founded in the person of Jesus Christ. On two occasions in its history, the trunk of this tree has branched off to produce these three different traditions within the one religion.

Remember: Catholics, Orthodox and Protestants are *all* members of the Christian faith because:

- they worship the same God
- they share certain basic beliefs, such as the Trinity, the Incarnation and the Resurrection.

Christianity: Areas of Disagreement

There are three main areas that divide Christians:

1. The Eucharist
   Catholic and Orthodox Christians accept the doctrine of *transubstantiation*. Protestants do not.
2. The Authority of the Pope
   Catholics believe that the pope is the head of the Church. Protestants do not.
3. The Ordination of Women
   Some Protestant Churches ordain women to the ministry. The Catholic and the Orthodox Churches do not.

Sectarianism

Prejudice is a preconceived opinion or bias against a person or thing.

One form of prejudice is *sectarianism*. This is a narrow-minded, hostile attitude towards people who do not share one's religious views.

Sectarianism can and has caused great suffering. Following the Reformation in the sixteenth century, Europe was torn apart by sectarian conflict. Many Catholics and Protestants were unwilling to respect each other's point of view and fought one another in a series of wars.

COMMUNITIES OF FAITH

Northern Ireland has experienced sectarian strife over the centuries. Since the 1960s, however, a number of Catholics and Protestants have worked to heal the deep divisions between people of different denominations through their involvement in the ecumenical movement.

Ecumenism

Ecumenism is the attempt to foster a sense of *togetherness* across the centuries-old divisions between Christians.

The purpose of the ecumenical movement is *not* to try to make all Christians the same. To do this would be to destroy what is distinctive in each tradition. Instead, it has two aims:

- to promote mutual respect and understanding between the different Christian traditions
- to encourage Christians to co-operate in the task of revealing the love of Christ to the world by what they say and do.

These aims can be achieved through:

- praying together, where possible
- dialogue between the members of the different *denominations* (i.e. branches of Christianity)
- co-operation on issues of moral/social importance.

Ecumenical Communities

Taizé

- Taizé is an ecumenical community located in southern France.
- The aims of this community are to work for Christian unity and to express the Christian message in modern terms.
- Taizé was founded in 1944 by a Protestant named Roger Shutz (died 2005).
- The community is made up of people from many nations and all three Christian traditions.
- All permanent members take three vows:
  1 to live a celibate life
  2 to share all their goods
  3 to accept the authority of the prior (community leader).

- Ecumenical prayer services are conducted in several languages three times each day: morning, noon and evening.
- Young people have flocked to Taizé from all over the world. There are now other groups who model themselves on Taizé dotted around the world.

Corrymeela

- Corrymeela is an ecumenical community located in Co. Antrim, Ireland.
- It was founded in 1965 by a Presbyterian minister named Ray Davey.
- The name Corrymeela means 'Hill of Harmony' and the community takes its ideal from this name.
- The community works to heal the political, social and religious divisions in Northern Ireland.
- It does so by providing a place where people from different religious denominations can spend time together and grow in understanding of one another.
- The community is open to people of all religions and those who do not belong to any.
- Important activities undertaken by the community include the international camp for young people and the 'Mixed Marriage Association', which supports marriages between people of different denominations.

The World Council of Churches

The World Council of Churches (WCC) was set up in Geneva in 1945. Its task is:

- to promote Christian unity
- to work for peace and justice.

The establishment of the WCC was an initiative by different Protestant churches. They believed that the divisions within Christianity were damaging its mission, for example:

- giving non-Christians a very poor impression of Christianity
- obstructing the spread of the Christian message and hindering the work of winning converts.

COMMUNITIES OF FAITH

The WCC holds a general assembly every six years. The delegates to the assembly discuss issues of common concern, such as:

- racism
- poverty
- environmental issues
- the plight of refugees
- the arms trade.

A practical expression of the WCC's concern for these matters was the setting up of the overseas aid agency Christian Aid.

At first the Catholic Church and the Orthodox Churches were not represented at the WCC, but the Orthodox Churches have been represented since 1961 and the Catholic Church has sent observers since 1968.

LEADERSHIP AND ORGANISATION OF COMMUNITIES OF FAITH

(Higher Level only)

Role of the Leader

A leader is someone who guides and influences others towards the achievement of some particular goal(s).

Religious leaders play an important role in communities of faith, though the exact nature of their leadership differs from one religion to the next. Depending on the particular community of faith, religious leaders can perform some or all of the following roles:

- interpreting the stories and teachings contained in sacred texts, and explaining their relevance to believers' lives today
- leading people in worship
- preserving the authentic doctrine (teachings) of the religion and guarding against heresy (false teachings)
- encouraging the handing on of traditions (accepted teachings and practices) from one generation to the next
- setting a good example for others to follow

- encouraging people to convert (change) and become members of their particular community of faith.

Examples of Leadership

The Rabbi in Judaism

The title *rabbi* means *my master* or *my teacher.*

A rabbi is someone employed by a Jewish community to have authority over the running of their synagogue. Rabbis are usually male, but some Jewish communities employ a female rabbi. A rabbi is *not* a priest. He/she is a lay person who has studied for several years to assume a leadership role in the Jewish community.

A rabbi conducts weddings and funeral services, visits the sick and may act as a chaplain to schools, hospitals or prisons. He or she also gives the sermon at the synagogue services held each Sabbath (i.e. Friday evening and Saturday morning). The *cantor* leads the congregation in singing the hymns and chanting prayers.

The Priest in the Catholic Church

The title *priest* comes from the Greek word *presbyteros,* meaning *elder.* A priest is a man who has been *ordained,* which means that he has received the sacrament of holy orders from a bishop.

A priest is expected to:

- offer spiritual leadership to his *parish* (local Christian community)
- administer the sacraments, e.g. celebrate mass, hear confessions and baptise new members
- give witness to the love of God by his presence and example, e.g. visit the sick, aid the homeless and counsel those in crisis
- explain the Church's teaching through sermons and/or discussion.

The Imam in Islam (Sunni Tradition)

The title *imam* comes from the Arabic word meaning *leader.*

An imam is the learned spiritual leader of a *mosque,* which is the religious, social and educational centre of a local Islamic community.

An imam is a layman, not a priest. He is selected for the position of imam because of his deep knowledge of the Qur'an and clear commitment to the Islamic way of life.

He gives the sermon and leads the prayers in the mosque. He also teaches the Qur'an to Muslim children. Muslim parents sometimes ask their imam to help them choose a name for their newborn child.

Types of Organisation in Christianity

Apostolic Mission

All baptised Christians are *equal* members of the Christian community. Every Christian shares in the responsibility of fulfilling the *apostolic mission*, which means making Jesus Christ known and drawing others to follow him by the example of their lives.

Episcopal and Non-Episcopal

The different Christian denominations (branches) organise themselves in one of two ways to fulfil the apostolic mission:

- *episcopal*: where there are bishops in authority over a Christian community
- *non-episcopal*: where there are no bishops in authority over a Christian community.

The Catholic Church, Church of Ireland and Orthodox Churches are episcopal.
The Baptist, Methodist and Presbyterian churches are non-episcopal.

Examples of Organisation

The Catholic Church

The Catholic Church is the largest Christian denomination with a worldwide membership of over one billion people.

All Catholics are equal in their membership of the Church, but they belong to one or other of the following categories:

- the *clergy*, which consists of all *ordained* members, i.e. those who have received the sacrament of holy orders and who, as a result, may administer the sacraments to others
- the *laity*, which consists of all *non-ordained members*.

The task of guiding the beliefs and moral actions of Catholics is the responsibility of the *Magisterium*, the teaching authority of the Catholic Church.

The Magisterium, strictly speaking, consists of the pope and the college of bishops under his leadership. The pope and the bishops are believed to be the direct successors of the original apostles who gathered around Jesus two thousand years ago.

The Catholic Church is said to be united through the power of the Holy Spirit under the leadership of the pope in Rome. The pope is acknowledged by Catholics as the visible head of Christ's Church and is given the title *Vicar of Christ* (meaning *Christ's representative on Earth*).

Each pope is elected within a few weeks of his predecessor's death by a group of the most senior clergymen, who are entitled to cast a vote. These senior clergymen are called *cardinals*. They hold a *conclave* (secret meeting), in which they choose the next pope.

Cardinals are appointed by the pope and act as his advisors. There is usually at least one cardinal in each country that has a substantial Catholic population.

Bishops are also appointed by the pope to care for the people of an area called a *diocese*.

Each diocese is divided into a number of *parishes* (local Christian communities), each of which usually has a priest who leads the laity in worship and ministers to their needs.

The Church of Ireland
The Church of Ireland is:

- a self-governing Christian denomination with about 375,000 members on the island of Ireland
- a member of the 70 million-strong international Anglican fellowship of independent churches
- in communion with the Anglican Church in England (the Church of England) but is completely autonomous (separate)
- led by the Protestant Archbishop of Armagh. It is *not* under the authority of the Archbishop of Canterbury.

Church of Ireland bishops attend the Lambeth Conference, which is held every ten years, to discuss important moral and religious issues with the leaders of other Anglican churches from around the world. Any decisions reached at the Lambeth Conference must then be debated and accepted by

COMMUNITIES OF FAITH

the governing bodies of the individual Anglican churches before they take effect.

The General Synod is the chief decision-making body of the Church of Ireland. It meets every year and consists of two parts:

- the House of Bishops (12 members)
- the House of Representatives (216 clergy and 432 laity).

Each diocese holds its own local synod once a year to elect the diocese's representatives to the General Synod.

At parish level, decisions are made by *select vestries*, i.e. groups of people who are elected each year by their local congregation.

Whereas the Catholic Church ordains only men and insists on their living celibate lives (being unmarried), the Church of Ireland ordains both men and women to the ministry and they may marry if they wish.

TABLE 1.3 Some Religious Groups in Ireland Today

Name of church or religious group	Title of leader
Catholic Church	Primate of All Ireland (Catholic)
Church of Ireland	Primate of All Ireland (Protestant)
Presbyterian Church	Moderator
Methodist Church	President
Jewish Community	Chief Rabbi
Islamic Community	No national leader: each mosque has its own imam
Baptist Church	President
Salvation Army	General
Society of Friends (Quakers)	None

Section B
Foundations of Religion

2 Christianity

THE LIFE OF JESUS: CONTEXT

Name

The part of the Middle East where the story of Jesus took place has had many names over the centuries.

TABLE 2.1

Land of Canaan	when Abraham and the Hebrews arrived there c. 1850 B.C.
Promised Land	after God made his covenant (sacred agreement) with Abraham and the Jews.
Israel (which means *God strives*). This is the name by which it is known today.	when it was ruled by King David and his successor Solomon.
Palestine. This is the name we shall use in this section.	after it was conquered by the Romans in the first century B.C.

Size

Total area: approximately 7,000 square miles.
Length (from north to south): about 150 miles.
Width (from east to west): between 30 and 50 miles.

Political Regions

As you can see from the map overleaf, the principal political regions of Palestine were:

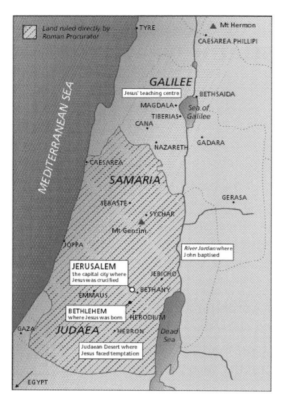

- Galilee in the north
- Samaria in the centre
- Judaea in the south.

The Romans, who ruled the area, allowed Palestine to exist as a united kingdom under the control of a Roman-appointed king until the death of Herod the Great in 4 B.C. After this the Emperor appointed a *procurator* (governor) to administer Samaria and Judaea, while allowing one of Herod's sons to serve as *tetrarch* (commander) of Galilee.

Community Life

People lived in one or other of the following communities:

- the old Jewish cities and towns (e.g. Jerusalem)
- the new Roman cities (e.g. Caesarea)
- small rural farming and fishing villages.

Jesus grew up in the old Jewish town of Nazareth in Galilee. Most Jews earned their living from manual labour – farming, fishing and craftwork.

A small professional elite, composed of educated people, did not do such manual work. These people were administrators, doctors, merchants and religious leaders.

Challenges

The climate and terrain made life difficult because:

CHRISTIANITY

- much of the landscape was sand and rock and therefore unsuitable for farming
- there were periodic droughts
- the sirocco (hot east winds) could strip away dry topsoil
- plagues of locusts could devour crops.

Roman Rule

The Roman emperor appointed a procurator (governor) named Pontius Pilate to govern Judaea and Samaria between A.D. 26 and 36.

His job was to:

- maintain order among 750,000 people
- keep the trade routes open
- ensure the full and prompt payment of taxes.

However, Pilate had only a garrison of 3,000 soldiers at his disposal to do all this. The key to his success in fulfilling his mission was twofold:

1 *threat elimination* – using an extensive network of spies to identify and swiftly eliminate anyone considered a threat to Roman rule
2 *rule by co-operation* – obtaining the co-operation of the Sanhedrin and enlisting its help in administering the provinces.

The Sanhedrin

The Sanhedrin was the ruling council of the Jewish religion. Based in Jerusalem, it was composed of seventy Jewish elders who elected a High Priest to oversee its activities. Its membership was divided into two rival groups – the Sadducees and the Pharisees (see pp 30–1).

The Romans allowed the Sanhedrin:

- to act as a court of law with powers to punish any Jews who broke their religion's laws
- to have its own armed force, the Temple guard, to enforce its decisions.

However, the Romans:

- could remove the High Priest from office if he displeased them and dictate who his successor would be

- refused to allow the Sanhedrin to inflict the death penalty.

Only the procurator could condemn a person to death.

Tax Collectors

As subjects of the Roman emperor, the Jews had to pay heavy taxes. A number of Jews were willing to supervise and collect these taxes. These *tax collectors* were despised and treated as social outcasts by most Jews. They were not allowed to hold any religious office or to give evidence in court.

This was because most Jews believed that tax collectors were traitors and thieves, as the Romans allowed them to keep for themselves a proportion of any taxes they had collected.

Jesus shocked many people by inviting a tax collector named Matthew to become an apostle.

Jewish Hopes

The Old Testament prophets promised that one day God would send someone who would unite and lead the Jewish people. The title given to this anticipated figure was *messiah*, from the Hebrew word *moshiach* meaning *anointed one*.

By the first century A.D., most Jews believed that the messiah would:

- free them from Roman occupation
- establish an independent Jewish kingdom
- reign over them with justice and bring peace and prosperity.

Reactions to Roman Rule

The Romans never let the Jews forget that Palestine was merely a small province of the vast Roman empire. The four most important groups within the Jewish community each reacted differently to Roman rule.

The Sadducees
- Composed of the High Priest, Temple priests and wealthy aristocrats.
- Rejected belief in life after death.
- Did not expect a messiah to come and free them from Roman rule.
- Accepted Roman rule, co-operated with the procurator and used their influence to help keep order.

The Pharisees
- Composed of lay religious teachers (called rabbis) who controlled the local synagogues.
- Believed in life after death.
- Expected a messiah to free them from Roman rule and establish an independent Jewish kingdom.
- Rejected Roman rule but did not actively oppose it.
- Devoted all their energies to rigorously practising their religion.

The Essenes
- Composed of men who underwent a three-year training period to become monks. They devoted their lives to prayer, fasting and study.
- Believed that they alone had the correct interpretation of Judaism's sacred texts.
- Expected two messiahs – one (a priest) who would restore the Temple and a second (a warrior) who would free them from Roman rule.
- Rejected Roman rule but did not actively oppose it.
- Separated themselves from the rest of society and established monasteries in remote desert areas.
- May have been the authors of the Dead Sea Scrolls.

The Zealots
- Composed of deeply religious Jews and may have been an off-shoot of the Pharisees.
- Rejected Roman rule and believed that violence was the only way to end it.
- Expected that the messiah would be a warrior king who would end foreign domination and restore the Jewish kingdom to what it had been in the time of King David.
- Staged several failed revolts led by men who claimed to be the messiah.
- Hated the Sadducees for working with the Romans and frequently carried out assassinations of them.

SOURCES FOR THE LIFE OF JESUS

Jesus of Nazareth did not leave any written account of his life and/or teachings. All information about him comes from sources written by others, both Christian and non-Christian.

Non-Christian Sources

TABLE 2.2

Origin	Document	Author	Date
Jewish	*Antiquities of the Jews*	Josephus (historian)	c. A.D. 90
	Talmud	Various rabbis	second century A.D.
Roman	*Letter to Emperor Trajan*	Pliny (procurator)	c. A.D. 110
	Annals	Tacitus (historian)	c. A.D. 115

TABLE 2.3

Information provided	Source
Jesus was a wise teacher and miracle worker who appealed to both Jews and gentiles	Josephus
He was condemned to death by Pontius Pilate	Josephus
This happened on the eve of the Jewish feast of Passover	Talmud
The execution happened during the reign of the Emperor Tiberius	Tacitus
Jesus's followers believed that he had risen from the dead	Josephus
His followers worshipped him as God	Pliny

Christian Sources

The New Testament consists of 27 books that were written in the latter half of the first century A.D. They are classified as follows:

TABLE 2.4

Title	Number	Purpose
Gospels	4	To record the life and teachings of Jesus.
Acts of the Apostles	1	To describe the expansion of Christianity.
Epistles	21	To offer advice to the early Christian communities and to clarify key teachings.
Book of Revelations	1	Predicts the triumph of God and the final judgment of human beings at the end of time.

- The earliest known complete manuscript of the New Testament is the Codex Sinaiticus (fourth century A.D.).
- The earliest known fragment of the New Testament is the Rylands Papyrus, a fragment of John's Gospel, dating from A.D. 134.

The Gospels
Meaning
- The word *gospel* means *good news*.
- There are four gospels: *Mark, Matthew, Luke* and *John*.
- The authors of the gospels are called *evangelists*, meaning *proclaimers of the good news*.

Importance
The gospels are our principal sources of information about the life of Jesus of Nazareth.

Dates
The first gospel to be written was Mark, circa A.D. 64. The last was John, circa A.D. 90.

Purpose
- To preserve vital information about Jesus.

- To correct any mistaken ideas about his teachings.
- To provide readings for Christian worship.

Focus

The gospels do not offer a biography of Jesus in the modern sense of the word. For example, they don't include a physical description of him, nor do they provide a day-by-day account of events in his life.

The evangelists were more concerned with explaining the *meaning* and *importance* of Jesus's life. They believed that he was the promised messiah (saviour) and wanted to persuade others to believe this too.

One story

There are four gospels.

Each gospel includes details that the others do not. For example: *Matthew* and *Luke* begin their accounts with the story of Jesus's birth, while *Mark* and *John* begin with the adult Jesus.

While they differ in certain details, all four gospels essentially tell the same story: the life, death and resurrection of Jesus. Each evangelist offers his own version of the story.

Why? Each gospel is written to meet the needs of a different Christian audience. For example:

- *Matthew* was written for those who had converted (changed) from Judaism to Christianity
- *Luke* was written for gentiles (non-Jews) and emphasised the idea that Jesus was the saviour of *all* people.

The Synoptics

The gospels of Mark, Matthew and Luke largely agree in their:

- outline of the main events in Jesus's life
- sequencing of these events
- wording of Jesus's statements.

It is because of these similarities that these three gospels are referred to as the *synoptics*: the word synoptic means *seen together*.

Mark was the first gospel to be written. The authors of Matthew and Luke both used Mark as a source when writing their own accounts. However, they also included material not found in Mark. Scholars believe that this other material came from the *Q* document.

The *Q* document (from the German word *quelle*, meaning source) is thought to have been a collection of Jesus's sayings which was written some time between A.D. 50 and 64. No copy of the *Q* document is known to have survived.

The Gospel of John
John was written after the synoptics, c. A.D. 90.
John differs from them in the following ways:

1 It did not copy material from either Mark or the Q document.
2 It does not mention the parables of Jesus and includes only a few of the miracle stories.
3 It offers a different sequence for certain events in Jesus's life, for example John places the cleansing of the Temple early in Jesus's ministry, whereas the synoptics state that it occurred later, during Holy Week.
4 It is primarily focused on the question of Jesus's identity, rather than on the events of his life. This is because by the end of the first century A.D. that was the question that most concerned Christians.

EARLY LIFE AND PUBLIC MINISTRY OF JESUS

The Nativity

TABLE 2.5

Meaning	From the Latin word *natus* meaning *the birth*, in this case the birth of Jesus.
Sources	The gospels of *Matthew* and *Luke*.
Account	These gospels were written separately, but they agree on the following details: • the story of Jesus's birth is set during the reign of King Herod the Great (died in 4 B.C.) • Jesus's mother was a young woman named Mary. She was a virgin who had been formally engaged to a carpenter named Joseph

TABLE 2.5 (contd.)

Account	• Jesus was conceived in Mary's womb, not through sexual intercourse with Joseph, but through the power of God. This is called 'the virginal conception' or 'the virgin birth' • Mary gave birth to Jesus in Bethlehem in Judaea • Jesus was given his name (derived from the Old Testament hero Joshua, meaning *saviour*) before his birth • Jesus, Mary and Joseph then settled in Nazareth in Galilee.
Differences	The accounts of Matthew and Luke differ in several ways. For example: • Only *Luke* tells of how the angel Gabriel appeared to Mary and told her that God had chosen her to be the mother of the messiah. This event is called the *Annunciation.* • *Luke* tells of how shepherds visited the infant Jesus, but does not mention the Magi (wise men). *Matthew* mentions the Magi but not the shepherds • only Matthew tells the story of how Herod ordered the *slaughter of the innocents* (male children aged two years or younger).
Purpose	Each evangelist wrote his version of the nativity story to help readers understand the *meaning* of Jesus's birth: • *Luke* mentioned the shepherds to show that Jesus had come to bring God's love and forgiveness to people of all social classes, rich and poor • *Matthew* told the story of the Magi to emphasise that Jesus had come to bring God's love and forgiveness to all people – Jews and gentiles.

TABLE 2.5 (contd.)

Date	The exact date of Jesus's birth is not recorded in the New Testament. The task of working out Jesus's birth date was given to a monk named Denis in the sixth century A.D. Most scholars now believe that Denis miscalculated. It is likely that Jesus was born sometime between 6 B.C. and 4 B.C. Why? • Herod the Great died in 4 B.C. Matthew says that he ordered the slaughter of the innocents (male children of up to two years of age). Therefore, Jesus would have had to have been born sometime between 6 B.C. and 4 B.C. • Matthew mentions a brilliant star which guided the Magi to the infant Jesus. Chinese astronomical records state that such a brilliant star appeared in the eastern sky in 5 B.C.

John the Baptist

John the Baptist was a cousin of Jesus. He was an *ascetic* (someone who lives a life of self-denial). He wore a robe made from camel hair and survived on a diet of locusts and wild honey.

He urged people to repent and be baptised in the river Jordan to show that their sins had been forgiven.

He was the *herald of the messiah*, i.e. the one who forewarned the people and prepared them for the coming of the messiah.

He reluctantly agreed to baptise Jesus, whom he recognised as the messiah.

John was imprisoned and executed by Herod Antipas, Tetrarch of Galilee.

The Temptations

After his baptism, Jesus went alone into the Judaean wilderness, where he fasted and prayed for forty days.

During this time, Satan tempted Jesus three times. On each occasion Jesus rejected Satan's offer.

TABLE 2.6

Temptations	Jesus's response
1 Jesus should use his power to turn stones into bread.	Rejects this. Says: *Man cannot live on bread alone.*
2 Jesus should forget about his mission and worship Satan instead.	Rejects this. Says: *You must worship the Lord your God and serve him alone.*
3 Jesus should use his power to impress people by throwing himself off the highest point in the Temple and have the angels save him.	Rejects this. Says: *You must not put the Lord your God to the test.*

After this Satan realised he had failed and left Jesus. But Satan did return on other occasions to tempt Jesus again.

The Personality of Jesus

The gospels portray Jesus as an extraordinary person who was uniquely good and remarkably charismatic.

Among his many qualities were:

- modesty and humility
- courage in the face of danger and intimidation
- shrewdness of judgment
- fairness and honesty
- matching words with deeds by always practising what he preached
- detestation of hypocrisy and corruption in all its forms.

CHRISTIANITY

Discipleship

The word *disciple* comes from the Latin *disciplus,* meaning a *student.*

To be a disciple of Jesus means learning from his example and following his way of life.

The New Testament teaches that becoming a disciple of Jesus means making a complete break with the way one has lived one's life up to that point. It demands a *metanoia,* meaning a *complete change of heart.*

The Apostles

Jesus had many disciples. However, within his wide circle of followers, he gathered a smaller group of twelve of his closest companions around him. They became known as the twelve *apostles* (from the Greek word meaning *to send forth*).

The apostles came from different backgrounds:

- Peter – a fisherman
- Matthew – a tax collector
- Simon – a zealot.

Christian scholars believe that Jesus chose twelve apostles because of the importance of this number for the Jews. There had originally been twelve tribes of Hebrews, each one descended from one of Jacob's sons. Jesus wanted the apostles to act as the foundation stone for a new community of believers, made up of both Jews and gentiles.

The Kingdom of God

Jesus's public ministry began with his baptism by John the Baptist. An important part of his mission was to proclaim the *Kingdom of God* (also referred to as the *Reign of God*). This is an idea that can be traced back to the Old Testament.

TABLE 2.7

Difficulty	Jesus never offered a precise definition of the Kingdom of God. Instead, he used various images and stories to illustrate its meaning and inspire his listeners to think hard about what it meant and what it demanded of them.
Meaning	The Kingdom of God is not a place on the map. Jesus taught that: • The Kingdom of God is *in the present*. Through the life and teaching of Jesus, the Kingdom of God has already come. It exists wherever God's love reigns in people's hearts and where they struggle to live their lives by God's standards. • The Kingdom of God is *in the future*. It exists as the ideal or perfect community in which people truly realise that they are all God's children, members of the one family, and live lives committed only to goodness, justice and peace. • The Kingdom of God is a very deep *mystery*. It is so profound that only God fully understands it. Although people can gain insight into it through prayer and good works, they can never hope to understand it fully.

The Beatitudes

Jesus declared that the Kingdom of God had arrived *in him*. He called on people to reform their lives in order to enter the Kingdom. In the *Beatitudes* (from the Latin *beati* meaning *happy* or *blessed*) he set out the qualities people need if they want to be members of the Kingdom of God.

These include:

- deep faith in God
- poverty of spirit
- purity of heart
- willingness to forgive and be merciful
- commitment to peace.

The Parables of Jesus

TABLE 2.8

Meaning	*A parable is an image or story in which a person illustrates some point of his/her message by using concrete examples drawn from everyday life.*
Motive	Story-telling was an important part of Jewish culture and it was an effective way of getting Jesus's message across to people.
Method	Jesus used images and examples drawn from farming, fishing and shepherding because these were the contexts with which his listeners were familiar.
Themes	The parables can be divided into four groups, each exploring an important theme in Jesus's teaching about the Kingdom of God. 1 *Description of God* 　Example: The Prodigal Son, *Luke* 15:8–32 2 *Guidance as to how one should behave in order to enter the Kingdom of God.* 　Example: The Talents, *Matthew* 25:14–30 3 *Teachings about how people should treat one another in the Kingdom of God.* 　Example: The Good Samaritan, *Luke* 10:25–37 4 *Warnings about the future day of judgment when God's Kingdom will come in all its fullness.* 　Example: The Weeds among the Wheat, *Matthew* 13:24–30
Interpretation	A parable works on two levels: • on the surface – as an interesting, easily remembered story • at a deeper level – Jesus invites his listeners to work out the meaning hidden within it and apply its message to their lives.

Example: The Good Samaritan
Luke 10:25–37

This is the story of how a Samaritan traveller cares for a Jewish man whom he finds unconscious by the roadside. The injured man has been viciously attacked, robbed and left for dead. The Samaritan tends to his wounds and pays for him to be nursed back to health.

The Samaritans were a people who lived in Samaria, the land between Judaea in the south of Palestine and Galilee in the north. Jews travelling between Judaea and Galilee would usually go across to the east bank of the river Jordan to avoid contact with the Samaritans (see *John* 4:9).

Samaritans were descended from Jews who had married foreigners (i.e. non-Jews) and there had been a quarrel between pure Jews and Samaritans for centuries. The Samaritans had built their own temple at Mount Gerazim and had their own version of the Tenakh.

By the time of Jesus, most Jews despised the Samaritans and had nothing to do with them.

Jesus shocked his Jewish listeners by making a Samaritan the hero of this story, but he did so to make an important point about the Kingdom of God.

There is no place for racial or religious hatred in God's kingdom. The neighbour whom God requires each person to love is *anyone in need*.

The Miracles of Jesus

TABLE 2.9

Meaning	*A miracle is a wonderful or awe-inspiring event that occurs solely as a result of God's direct action.* The first-century Jewish historian Josephus described Jesus as a *doer of wonderful deeds*, i.e. one who worked miracles. The gospels record thirty-five different occasions when Jesus performed a miracle.

Types	There are four types of miracle recorded in the gospels:
	 1 *Healing miracles*
	     Example: The Healing of a Paralytic
	 2 *Exorcisms* (i.e. casting out demons)
	     Example: The Gadarene Demoniac

TABLE 2.9 (contd.)

Types	3 *Nature miracles*
	  Example: The Calming of a Storm
	4 *Restorations to Life*
	  Example: The Raising of the Widow's Son

Example	*A Healing Miracle* In *Luke* 5:12–14 Jesus not only healed a man afflicted by leprosy but actually *touched* him. Lepers were social outcasts who were ordered to keep apart from other people because their disease was so contagious. Jesus did something that no one else would have dared to do. He showed that while people may have rejected this man because of his illness, God had not. Jesus's actions revealed the love of God reaching out to and embracing people who were abandoned and suffering.
Need	Without clear evidence of Jesus's power over sin, suffering and death, his preaching about the Kingdom of God would have been generally dismissed by his Jewish audience. This was because: • most Jews at that time regarded physical suffering as a punishment from God for the sins one had committed • they would only believe that a person's sins had been forgiven if he/she was cured • by healing a person Jesus demonstrated that his authority to forgive sins and his power to heal came from God and that what he preached to them was true.
Motive	Jesus worked miracles for three reasons: • to strengthen the faith of those people who *already* believed in him • to reveal God's power in order to show people that the Kingdom of God had begun *in him* • to demonstrate God's *unlimited love* for each and every human being, regardless of their race or religion.

PASSION, DEATH AND RESURRECTION OF JESUS

Holy Week

This is the title given to the last week of Jesus's public ministry, set in spring, sometime during the years A.D. 30–33.

An Outline of Events

Sunday
Jesus arrived in Jerusalem seated on a colt and was welcomed by cheering crowds.

Monday
Jesus went to the Temple and denounced the traders and money-changers. He overturned their stalls and drove them out of the Temple. The Pharisees and the Sadducees in the Sanhedrin plotted to kill Jesus.

Tuesday
Jesus taught in the Temple and was asked some leading questions intended to trap him:

- by the Pharisees (about his authority and about his views on Roman taxation)
- by the Sadducees (about his views on life after death).

Wednesday
Judas Iscariot, one of Jesus's apostles, went to the Jewish authorities with an offer to betray Jesus so that he could be arrested quietly.

Thursday
Jesus shared an evening meal with his disciples. Judas left early. Later, in the Garden of Gethsemane, Judas arrived with the Temple police, who arrested Jesus. Judas identified him for them.

Friday
During the early hours Jesus was interrogated by the Sanhedrin and later put on trial by the Roman procurator, Pontius Pilate. Jesus was scourged and

condemned to death by crucifixion. He was nailed to an upright cross and suffered an agonising death. His body was buried in a tomb nearby.

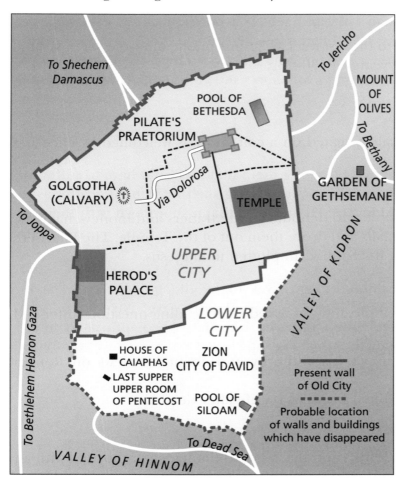

Palm Sunday
Jesus arrived in Jerusalem as preparations were under way for the annual feast of Passover. Most Jews believed that Passover was the time when the long-awaited messiah would reveal himself.

Jesus was enthusiastically welcomed by a large crowd of Jewish pilgrims as he entered Jerusalem:

- they waved palm branches in salute
- they acclaimed Jesus as *King of Israel*

- they shouted '*Hosanna*' (meaning *save now*).

Most Jews expected that the messiah would be a great warrior who would free them from Roman rule and set up a powerful, independent Jewish kingdom just like King David had in ancient times.

However, Jesus made it clear that he had no such political ambitions. He demonstrated this by entering Jerusalem seated on a colt – a humble animal of peace – not a war horse.

Conflict with the Jewish Authorities

Jesus shocked his disciples by telling them that he would have to suffer and die. He had made powerful enemies among such influential groups as the Pharisees and the Sadducees. He believed that a showdown with them was unavoidable.

Jesus and the Pharisees

The Pharisees considered themselves to be the greatest experts on religious matters. While some supported Jesus (e.g. Nicodemus and Joseph of Arimathea), most opposed him. Jesus had infuriated many Pharisees by criticising their *legalism* (harsh and excessive devotion to the precise letter of their religion's 613 laws).

Pharisees' accusations against Jesus

- Jesus committed blasphemy by claiming the power to forgive sins.
- His powers to work miracles came from Satan.
- When he healed people he was breaking the laws forbidding work on the Sabbath.
- He was unfit to be called *rabbi* because he mixed with sinners, outcasts and non-Jews.

Jesus's response to them

- As the Son of Man he had the authority to forgive sins.
- His power to do so came from God.
- He was the Lord of the Sabbath.
- His mission was to reveal God's love to *all* people. All were invited to enter the Kingdom of God.

Jesus and the Sadducees
The Sadducees controlled the Temple and the office of High Priest. They seem to have ignored Jesus until he challenged their activities. Jesus had witnessed how the money-changers and traders in the Court of Gentiles were exploiting devout pilgrims by over-charging them. He expelled them from the Temple's precincts in full view of large numbers of pilgrims.

The leading Sadducees were furious with Jesus because:

- he had publicly exposed the corrupt practices they had allowed to thrive (and may have benefited from) in Judaism's holiest site
- he had clearly demonstrated their hypocrisy and failure to uphold the high standards that they demanded of everyone else.

Reaction of both to Jesus
Both the Pharisees and the Sadducees agreed that they could not allow Jesus to go on challenging their authority. Since he could neither be intimidated nor bought off, they concluded that he had to be killed.

Betrayal

The Pharisees and the Sadducees were afraid to arrest Jesus in daylight for fear of triggering a riot in Jerusalem. They decided to arrest him after dark, out of public view, and then hand him over to the Romans before the general population knew what had happened.

However, the Sanhedrin's leaders did not know where Jesus was staying and needed inside help to capture him. This was provided by Judas Iscariot, one of the apostles, who told them when and where they could find him.

There have been two reasons advanced for Judas's betrayal:

1 he was a greedy opportunist who had lost patience with Jesus and sold him out to make money and gain influential new friends
2 he was not treacherous but misguided. He may have believed that he had to force Jesus to convince the Sanhedrin that he was the messiah and then go on to establish the independent Jewish kingdom so many hoped to see.

Arrest

After sharing a meal with his disciples on Holy Thursday evening, Jesus went with them to pray in the Garden of Gethsemane. There he was arrested by Temple guards who had been led there by Judas. At this point all the disciples fled, leaving Jesus to face his ordeal alone.

Interrogation by the Sanhedrin

Jesus was brought before the Sanhedrin. This was a court of inquiry rather than a formal trial. Jesus was not given a fair hearing:

- he was beaten both before and during his interrogation
- he was not charged with any particular offence
- he was questioned in the hope that he would say something that would allow them to accuse him of an offence punishable by death.

For some time Jesus remained silent. He knew that the outcome had already been decided. The Sanhedrin was only trying to decide what charge could be made against Jesus that would ensure his execution by the Romans.

The High Priest, Caiaphas, asked Jesus directly if he was the messiah. When Jesus responded 'I am', his enemies condemned him for committing blasphemy and decided to accuse him of being a dangerous political trouble-maker.

Trial

On Good Friday morning, a delegation from the Sanhedrin brought Jesus to the Antonia Fortress to be tried by the Roman procurator, Pontius Pilate. They claimed that Jesus was guilty of treason because he had:

- proclaimed himself to be the messiah
- told people not to pay their taxes
- disturbed the peace and threatened to lead a revolt.

If found guilty of treason, Jesus would be sentenced to death by crucifixion.

Pilate examined the evidence they offered and concluded that Jesus was *innocent* of these charges.

CHRISTIANITY

Not wishing to offend the Sanhedrin, Pilate attempted to unload this matter onto Herod Antipas, tetrarch of Galilee. However, Herod only sent Jesus back to Pilate, though he allowed his guards to beat Jesus and dress him in a purple robe (to make fun of claims that Jesus was a king).

Pilate believed that Jesus posed no threat to Roman rule but, in order to satisfy the Sanhedrin, he had Jesus scourged (flogged). However, the Sanhedrin delegates still insisted on the death penalty.

Pilate offered the crowd a choice between releasing Jesus and a violent rebel named Barabbas. To his surprise they chose to release Barabbas. When he still hesitated to condemn Jesus, the Sanhedrin delegation threatened to report Pilate to the Emperor Tiberius for failing to execute an enemy of the empire. At this point Pilate gave in and ordered Jesus to be crucified.

Crucifixion

Crucifixion was an agonising death intended to deter people from challenging the authority of Rome. Jesus was forced to carry the wooden crossbeam through the streets of Jerusalem to his place of execution on a hill outside the city walls – *Golgotha* (the place of the skull).

He was nailed to the cross through his wrists and feet. Above his head Pilate ordered a plaque to be placed reading 'Jesus of Nazareth, King of the Jews'.

Jesus endured six hours of torment before he finally died from a combination of suffocation, exhaustion and blood loss.

Burial

To ensure that Jesus was dead, Roman guards pierced his side with a spear, puncturing his lungs.

Joseph of Arimathea claimed the body for burial in a little tomb cut out of rock and located nearby. Since the Sabbath was approaching, the burial itself was a hurried affair. The tomb was sealed by rolling a large stone across its entrance. The women disciples agreed to return after the Sabbath to embalm the corpse properly.

Resurrection

TABLE 2.10

Setting	Early on Easter Sunday morning a group of women disciples led by Mary Magdalene went to the tomb to embalm Jesus's corpse.
Discovery	They discovered that the stone covering the entrance had been rolled back and that the tomb was empty. Then they heard an announcement that Jesus had risen from the dead. Mary Magdalene met the risen Jesus in the garden nearby.
Reaction	The women went to tell the apostles, who were in hiding. At first the apostles did not believe them. Peter and John went to the tomb and found it empty.
NB	The Gospels make it clear that no one actually claimed to have seen Jesus rising from the dead. Their accounts deal with what occurred afterwards.
Appearances	According to the New Testament a large number of people actually met and spoke with the risen Jesus. Each appearance followed this pattern: • Jesus appeared among his disciples and reassured his astonished followers by saying 'Peace be with you' (*John* 20:21) • their initial shock faded and was replaced by an inner peace and joy • he told them to 'Go and make disciples of all nations' (*Matthew* 28:19).
Glorified life	Jesus was/is alive but not in the same way as before his death. He had not been restored to his former earthly life as had Lazarus and the widow's son. Jesus was/is no longer limited by the physical laws that limit all human actions. For example, Jesus could: • be physically present in two places at the same time • appear at will and disappear again.

Through his resurrection Jesus was *transformed* and *glorified* (i.e. he lives a completely new, mysterious and higher form of life).

FAITH IN JESUS CHRIST

The Ascension

Forty days after Easter Sunday, Jesus appeared to his disciples for one last time before returning to Heaven. He promised them that, although he would no longer be physically present among them, he would send the Holy Spirit to guide and strengthen them.

Pentecost

Ten days later, the disciples gathered in Jerusalem to celebrate Pentecost (the Jewish harvest festival). There the Holy Spirit came upon them 'like tongues of fire' (*Acts* 2:3), giving them the courage and strength they would need to complete the work Jesus had begun. The disciples began publicly preaching that Jesus was the messiah and that he had risen, and began healing the sick in Jesus's name.

Reaction of the Jewish Authorities

The Sanhedrin became alarmed by the rapid increase in the number of *Christians* (followers of Jesus Christ). They arrested a Christian leader named Stephen and tried him for blasphemy. The trial ended in a riot and Stephen was stoned to death.

Many Christians decided to leave Palestine and moved to other Jewish communities scattered throughout the Roman empire.

Paul of Tarsus

The Christian message spread quickly throughout the Mediterranean region in the first century A.D. The most outstanding Christian *missionary* (one who is sent to spread a religion) was *Paul* (or, in Hebrew, *Saul*) of Tarsus.

Paul had been a devout Pharisee who had at one time persecuted

Christians. While journeying from Jerusalem to Damascus Paul had an extraordinary experience that led him to convert to Christianity.

Paul was then hunted by the Jewish authorities who accused him of *heresy* (spreading false ideas about God). However, Paul escaped and set out on the first of three great missionary journeys around the eastern Mediterranean. He set up numerous new Christian communities. He wrote *epistles* (letters offering advice to his fellow Christians), which were later included in the New Testament.

Paul was uniquely well-equipped for his mission because:

- he was Jewish by religion
- he enjoyed Roman citizenship
- he spoke Aramaic, Greek, Hebrew and Latin, so he could communicate with both Jews and gentiles.

Paul was finally arrested by the Roman authorities and executed on the orders of Emperor Nero in A.D. 64.

The Council of Jerusalem

The first general council of Christian leaders was held in Jerusalem in A.D. 49. It was called to decide a question that was sharply dividing Christians: *did a person have to become a Jew* (and therefore be circumcised, if male) *before becoming a Christian* (by baptism)?

Paul won Peter and the majority present over to his solution: new converts did *not* have to become Jews before becoming Christians. All that was needed to become a Christian was repentance for one's sins, and baptism.

This decision by the Council of Jerusalem severed Christianity's link with Judaism and clearly established Christianity as a *separate* world religion.

Persecution

By the mid-first century A.D., the Roman authorities had grown highly suspicious of Christians for several reasons:

- Christians refused to acknowledge the emperor as a god or to worship him
- they would not attend the bloodthirsty games in the arena and encouraged others to boycott them
- they refused to enlist in the armed forces.

Also, unfounded rumours began to circulate that Christians engaged in cannibalism.

When a fire destroyed much of the city of Rome in A.D. 64, the Emperor Nero (who may have been responsible) blamed the Christians. He launched a vicious persecution involving torture and crucifixion. Both Peter and Paul were put to death, along with hundreds of others.

However, the Christian religion survived this and other periods of persecution. Finally, the Emperor Constantine granted Christians freedom of worship in A.D. 313. By then, Christianity had spread as far as Ireland, Ethiopia, India and China.

The Titles of Jesus

(Higher Level only)

Messiah/Christ

The title *Messiah* comes from the Hebrew *Moshiach*, meaning *anointed one*, i.e. someone who has been chosen by God to carry out an important task.

By the first century A.D., most Jews hoped that the Messiah would be a warrior king who would:

- bring God's peace and justice among them
- free them from foreign domination
- set up a new Jewish kingdom.

Jesus was not the kind of Messiah that most Jews were expecting.

When the Bible was first translated from Hebrew into Greek, the Greek word used in place of the Hebrew Messiah was *christos*. From this we get the title *Christ* (also meaning *anointed one*). Therefore, *Jesus Christ* means *Jesus the Messiah*.

The Jewish people believe that the Messiah has yet to come. Christians, however, believe that in Jesus of Nazareth the Messiah/Christ *has arrived* and that *he will return again at the end of time.*

Son of Man

This is the title that Jesus used to describe himself in the Gospel of Mark. It is the only specific title that Jesus is recorded as having directly applied to himself.

In the Old Testament book of Daniel, the title Son of Man was used to refer to the Messiah.

Jesus claimed that he was the Son of Man because he could do things that only God could do, such as forgive people's sins.

Lord

For the Jews, God's name was *Yahweh*. However, they considered God's name to be so holy that it should never be spoken. So out of respect they substituted the title *Lord* for God's name.

The first Christians began to refer to Jesus as *the Lord*. This was because they believed that Jesus possessed authority over sin and power over death that belonged only to God.

Son of God

Sometimes first-century Jews referred to an exceptionally good person as a *son of God*.

By the time the Gospel of John came to be written at the end of the first century A.D. the early Christians had had time to reflect on Jesus's many references to God as his *Father*.

They realised that Jesus is not simply *a* son of God. All Jesus had said and done had shown him to have a totally unique relationship with God, his Father, so much so that he *shares* in God's very nature.

Jesus is not merely *a* son of God. Jesus is *the* Son of God.

Section C
Foundations of Religion

3 Judaism

MEANING

Judaism means *the religion of the Jews* (originally known as the Hebrews).

PLACE OF ORIGIN

The area now known as the state of Israel.

FOUNDERS

The Jews refer to the founding fathers of Judaism as the *patriarchs*. The most important patriarchs were *Abraham* and *Moses*.

Abraham

According to *Genesis* 12:1–2, God called on Abraham to lead his people, first known as the Hebrews and later as the Jews, to leave Mesopotamia (modern Iraq) and settle in the Promised Land (modern Israel).

God made a *covenant* (sacred agreement) with Abraham and his descendents. If they faithfully worshipped him and kept his laws, then he would guarantee their ownership of the Promised Land.

At first the Jews believed that each nation had its own god. In time they came to believe that there is only one God. Judaism became the world's first *monotheistic* religion.

Moses

When famine struck the Promised Land (c. 1700 B.C.), many Jews emigrated to Egypt. Although welcomed at first, they were later forced into slavery. After suffering three centuries of oppression, God finally chose Moses to lead the Jews to freedom.

God spoke to Moses in the form of a bush that was on fire but was not burned up. Moses gained the courage to confront the Egyptian pharaoh (king) and demand that he release the Jews. When the pharaoh refused, God sent a series of plagues, which forced him to set them free.

The great movement of the Jews back to the Promised Land is called the *Exodus* (the going forth). During this journey, God renewed his covenant with the Jews.

If they were faithful to God's laws (summarised in the *Ten Commandments* given to Moses), then God would once more guarantee their ownership of the Promised Land.

It took the Jews another two hundred years before they finally defeated those who also laid claim to the Promised Land. They established the kingdom of *Israel* (meaning *God strives*) with its capital Jerusalem, where they built a temple to house the *Ark of the Covenant* (a casket containing the stone tablets on which the Ten Commandments had been written).

BELIEFS

TABLE 3.1

God	The Tenakh teaches that God is the all-knowing, all-powerful creator of the universe who is completely good and loving.
	The Hebrew name for God is *Yahweh*, but out of respect this name is not spoken. Instead, God is usually referred to as *Adonai*, meaning *Lord*.
Covenant	The *covenant* is the *sacred agreement* that God first made with Abraham and his descendants and later renewed with Moses and the Jews after their escape from Egypt.
	In it God promised the Jews that if they faithfully worshipped him and followed his laws, he would guarantee their ownership of the Land of Canaan – or what the Jews call the *Promised Land* (modern Israel).
	A symbol of this covenant is the ritual of male

TABLE 3.1 (contd.)

	circumcision. This marks Jews as God's *chosen people* and reminds them of their duty to remain faithful to that covenant.
Prophets	This does *not* mean people who can accurately predict future events. It refers to Jewish holy men who in ancient times received messages from God, which they then preached to their people. Famous prophets included Amos, Elijah, Jeremiah and Isaiah. They reminded the Jews of their duty to love God and follow his commandments.
Messiah	Following their return from exile in Babylon, the Jews were unable to preserve their independence from foreign powers. Over the centuries they were conquered by the Persians, Greeks and Romans in succession. Their prophets told them that God had promised to send them a leader who would: • be a descendent of King David • free them from foreign domination • restore Israel's greatness • bring about an era of peace and prosperity for the whole world. The leader chosen by God to fulfil this mission was given the title *messiah* (meaning *anointed one*). Jews believe that the messiah has yet to come. Christians believe Jesus of Nazareth was the messiah and that he will return again at the end of time.

SACRED TEXT

TABLE 3.2

Title	The *Tenakh* This title comes from the initial letters of each of its three sections: *T*, *N* and *K*.
Date	Initially, important stories and doctrines were passed on by oral tradition from one generation to the next. From about 1000 B.C. onwards these stories and doctrines were written down. However, they were not established in their final form until the first century A.D.
Oldest Complete Manuscript	Known as the *Dead Sea Scrolls*; discovered in 1947. So called because they were found stored in clay jars hidden in caves in the Qumran wilderness near the Dead Sea. Had been hidden there in the mid-first century A.D. to prevent them being destroyed by the Romans. May have been written by the Essenes.
Content	Consists of thirty-nine books, all written in Hebrew, gathered together into one volume. Can be divided into three sections: • *Torah* • *Nevi'im* • *Ketuvim*. The *Torah* (or *Pentateuch*). Translates as the *Law*. Consists of five books: *Genesis, Exodus, Leviticus, Numbers* and *Deuteronomy*. Believed to have been given directly by God to Moses and so considered to be the holiest part of the Tenakh. Contains: the story of the Jews from Abraham until their return to the Promised Land; and religious laws governing worship and daily life.

TABLE 3.2 (contd.)

	The *Nevi'im* Translates as the *Prophets*. Consists of eight books telling the story of the Jews after their return to the Promised Land. The *Ketuvim* Translates as the *Writings*. Consists of the books of *Proverbs* (wise sayings) and *Psalms* (songs and poems written to praise God's goodness).

JUDAISM TODAY

(Higher Level only)

Worldwide

There are an estimated 18 million Jews worldwide. Approximately 25 per cent live in Israel and 30 per cent in the USA; the remainder are scattered across the globe.

Ireland

There have been Jews living in Ireland for many centuries. The earliest documentary evidence mentions the arrival of five Jewish merchants in Ireland in the eleventh century.

By the beginning of the sixteenth century, a small number of Jews had settled in the Munster region following their expulsion from Portugal. In 1555, William Annyas was elected Mayor of Youghal, Co. Cork.

By the twentieth century, Jews were participating fully in all walks of life. Robert Briscoe was twice elected Lord Mayor of Dublin (1956 and 1961), an achievement repeated by his son Ben in 1988. Gerald Goldberg became Lord Mayor of Cork in 1977.

The earliest record of a synagogue in Ireland dates from 1660. Today there are six synagogues operating in Ireland – four in Dublin, one in Belfast and one in Cork.

The Jewish population in Ireland peaked at 5,500 in the late 1940s. Today it stands at about 1,700.

FAITH IN PRACTICE

(Higher Level only)

Kashrut

All Jews are expected to follow a special diet. *Kashrut* is the name given to the laws set out in *Leviticus* 17, which state:

- what can be eaten by Jews
- what they are forbidden to eat
- how permitted foods should be prepared.

Permitted food is referred to as *kosher*. Examples of kosher:

- fish with fins and scales
- meat from animals that both chew the cud *and* have cloven (split) hooves.

Pigs have cloven hooves but do not chew the cud. As a result, Jews are not permitted to eat pig meat.

All animals deemed kosher must be killed according to the rules of *shechita*. This involves slitting the animal's throat with only one cut so as to minimise its pain. Then the animal is entirely drained of its blood.

Separate utensils must always be used when preparing meat and dairy products.

Jews believe that faithfully following the laws concerning food helps to preserve their distinct religious identity and encourages them to obey all of God's laws.

Seder

The *Seder* is the Jewish ritual meal held to celebrate the Feast of Passover. It always follows the same set pattern that has been handed down over the centuries.

- In preparation for the Seder, Jewish families remove all traces of *hametz* (leavened/yeast bread) from homes. Special plates, glassware and cutlery that have had no previous contact with yeast bread are used.

JUDAISM

- The Seder itself begins with the head of the household saying a prayer called the *Kiddush*. Everyone takes parsley which has been dipped in salt water. The head of the household then breaks the *matzah* (a loaf of unleavened bread) and shares it out among those present.
- During the meal, wine is drunk with the food, but one glass of wine is poured but left untouched. This symbolises (represents) the belief that, at some future time, the prophet Elijah will return and announce the arrival of the Messiah.
- The youngest person present then asks: 'Why is this night different from all other nights?' The head of the household responds by reading the story of the Passover and the Exodus, telling of how God freed their ancestors from slavery in Egypt.

DIVISIONS

(Higher Level only)

Modern Judaism has four main branches:

- Orthodox
- Progressive
- Conservative
- Hasidic.

Orthodox

Orthodox Jews see themselves as the only faithful practitioners of the ancient religion of Israel. They claim to have been the only ones to have preserved unchanged its teachings and rituals over the centuries.

Orthodox Jews are required to:

- strictly follow the 613 *mitzvot* (commandments) of the Torah
- accept the interpretation of these mitzvot as set down in the *Talmud* (ancient commentary on the Torah)
- conduct all religious services in Hebrew
- observe all the religious rituals (festivals and rites of passage) with great devotion.

Further:

- women and men must be seated separately during worship in the synagogue
- women cannot become rabbis.

Progressive

The Progressive tradition in Judaism began in Europe in the late eighteenth century, when some countries began to ease the restrictions that had prevented Jews from playing a full role in society.

Unlike Orthodox Jews, Progressive Jews believe that the Torah must be understood as people's interpretation of God's word at a particular time and place in human history. Its teachings should be interpreted to take into account the changes that have occurred since the Torah was first written.

Progressive Jews have relaxed and changed certain laws relating to diet and worship in the synagogue to suit modern life. For example:

- men and women are not seated separately during worship in the synagogue
- girls undergo the *bat mitzvah* (which is equivalent to the bar mitzvah for boys)
- women may be ordained as rabbis.

Conservative

Conservative Judaism began in North America in the 1940s. Its members sought a middle way between Orthodox and Progressive forms of Judaism.

Conservative Jews hold firmly to all the essential traditions of Judaism while at the same time accepting certain elements of the Progressive approach. For example:

- interpreting the Torah in a way that meets the realities of modern society
- ordaining women as rabbis.

Hasidic

Hasid means *pious (dutiful) one*. The Hasidic movement in Judaism was started in the eighteenth century by Rabbi Israel Baal Shem Tov (d. 1760).

Hasidic Jews are instantly recognisable by their style of dress. Men grow long beards and long curling locks of hair either side of their heads. They wear distinctive black clothing and wide-brimmed hats.

The Hasidic tradition:

- demands literal faithfulness to the words of the Torah
- places greater emphasis on the enthusiastic and joyful praise of God than on the scholarly study and discussion of his teachings
- teaches that its leaders (called *rebbe*) possess greater gifts of insight into religious matters than are granted by God to rabbis.

4 Islam

MEANING

Islam is an Arabic word meaning *peace through submission to the revealed will of Allah.*

Muslim is an Arabic word meaning *one who submits*. It refers to a follower of Islam.

PLACE OF ORIGIN

The city of *Makkah* (also known as *Mecca*) in the Arabian peninsula (modern *Saudi Arabia*).

FOUNDER

Muhammad (the name means *highly praised*) was born in Makkah around A.D. 570. Orphaned at an early age, he was raised by his uncle and worked on camel caravans between the great trade centres of the Middle East.

As a young man he became business manager to a rich widow named Khadijah. They fell in love, married and had six children – two sons (both of whom died in childhood) and four daughters.

As a businessman, Muhammad was not only successful but also highly respected and known as *Al-Amin* (which means *trustworthy*).

Muhammad grew increasingly troubled by the corruption and injustice he witnessed in Makkah. He spent many hours praying and fasting alone in a cave on Mount Hira.

In A.D. 610 an event occurred that became known as the *Night of Power and Excellence*. Muhammad is said to have received a revelation from *Allah* (the Arabic word for *God*). The archangel Gabriel is said to have appeared and told Muhammad that he would be the *Prophet of Allah*, i.e. the one who would tell people the will of God.

In A.D. 613 Muhammad received another revelation, after which he began publicly preaching in Makkah. He said that people should:

- abandon polytheism
- believe in Allah
- treat one another fairly
- care for the sick and poor.

Muhammad angered Makkah's business and religious leaders by demanding that all idols should be removed from the *Kaaba* (which means the *House of God*). He said that the Kaaba should be used exclusively for the worship of Allah. However, these idols attracted many pilgrims to Makkah, and Muhammad was seen as a threat to the huge profits that were made from them by certain powerful people. He and his followers suffered increasing persecution as a result of his stand.

In A.D. 622 Muhammad and his followers left Makkah and moved to *Madinah* (which means *city of the prophet*). This event is known as the *Hijrah* or *Hegira* (meaning *the departure*).

(**N.B.** Muslims begin their calendar with the Hijrah. The year A.D. 622 is the first year of the Muslim calendar.)

In time, Muhammad became ruler of Madinah and was referred to as the *Rasul* (*Messenger of Allah*).

Muhammad fought several successful battles against his opponents and finally captured Makkah in A.D. 630. He immediately reformed its government and cleansed the Kaaba of idols.

By A.D. 631 Islam had spread across all of Arabia. Muhammad fell ill and died the following year. Within a century of his death, Islam had spread as far as Spain in the west and India in the east. Today, one-fifth of the world's population is Muslim.

SACRED TEXT

TABLE 4.1

Title	The *Qur'an* (pronounced Koran), meaning *that which is to be read*.
Date	Written in the mid-seventh century A.D., about twenty years after Muhammad's death.
Content	Contains 114 *surahs* (chapters), written in Arabic, which set out: • the basic beliefs of Islam • clear and strict guidelines as to how Muslims should live • punishments for wrongdoing.
Importance	Muslims believe that the Qur'an is literally the word of God. They are taught to treat every copy of it with great respect: for example, the Qur'an should never be left lying on the ground. The Qur'an rivals the Bible as the world's most widely read book.

BELIEFS

The key doctrines of Islam are known as the *five articles of faith*.

1. There is only one God, who is named *Allah*.
2. Angels are Allah's messengers.
3. The Qur'an is the final and complete revelation of Allah.
4. Muhammad is the last and the greatest prophet of Allah.
5. There will be a final day of judgment, when Allah will reward the good and punish the wicked.

Muslims are expected to uphold these beliefs in their daily lives by practising the *five pillars of faith*.

ISLAM

THE FIVE PILLARS

All Muslims are obliged to fulfil the five pillars of faith.

TABLE 4.2

1st Pillar	**Shahadah** To recite the following creed five times each day: *There is no God but Allah and Muhammad is his prophet.*
2nd Pillar	**Salat** To pray at set times each day and to attend a mosque for communal prayer on Friday.
3rd Pillar	**Zakat** To give alms (charity) to the poor, either voluntarily or by state deduction, of one-fortieth of one's earnings.
4th Pillar	**Saum** To fast during the daylight hours of Ramadan.
5th Pillar	**Hajj** To go on pilgrimage to Makkah at least once in one's lifetime.

DIVISIONS

(Higher Level only)

Following Muhammad's death, the rival factions among his followers agreed to choose a *caliph* (successor to Muhammad).

The first four caliphs were:

- Abu Bakr (d. 634)
- Umar (d. 644)
- Uthman (d. 656)
- Ali (d. 661).

After Ali's death (he had been Muhammad's son-in-law), a bitter dispute broke out about who should succeed him as caliph.

Two groups formed:

- the *Sunni* (orthodox) Muslims, who accepted the next caliph
- the *Shia* (*Shi'at Ali* — Party of Ali), who rejected the next caliph and followed the descendents of Ali.

Sunnis and Shias have been separate groups ever since and have fought one another at different times over the centuries.

One significant area of disagreement concerns the Qur'an:

- Sunnis believe that the Qur'an is complete and unaltered
- some Shias believe that the Qur'an was altered by the Sunnis, who removed any verses from the text that supported the Shia position.

ISLAM TODAY

(Higher Level only)

Worldwide

Islam is the world's second largest and fastest growing religion, with an estimated 1.2 billion members worldwide.

The majority of Muslims (about 90 per cent) are Sunni, while the remainder are Shia.

Shias are the dominant group in Iran and Pakistan.

Islam's three holiest sites are the cities of Makkah (Mecca), Madinah and Jerusalem.

Ireland

There are approximately 20,000 Muslims living in Ireland.

There are mosques in Dublin, Cork, Galway and Belfast.

The first mosque in Ireland, opened in 1975, was in Harrington Street, Dublin. Another was opened in 1983 on the South Circular Road, Dublin to meet the needs of the growing Islamic community.

The first Muslim national school (primary level) was opened in 1990 and moved to its current site at Clonskeagh, Dublin in 1993.

In 1992, Dr Moosajee Bhamjee became the first Muslim to be elected to the Oireachtas as a TD for Co. Clare.

The Islamic Cultural Centre was opened at Clonskeagh in 1996.

5 Buddhism

MEANING

Buddhism is a set of beliefs based on the teachings of the Buddha.

Buddha is a title that means the *enlightened one*. It was given to the founder of Buddhism – Siddhartha Gautama.

PLACE OF ORIGIN

The foothills of the Himalayan Mountains, on the borders of modern India and Nepal.

FOUNDER

Siddhartha Gautama was probably born around 565 B.C. (though some recent scholarship suggests he was born around 480 B.C.). He was an Indian prince who enjoyed a luxurious lifestyle while he was growing up and was completely sheltered from the harsh realities of life. He married Princess Yosodhara and they had a son. His life seemed complete.

By the age of thirty, however, Siddhartha had grown dissatisfied. He felt that there must be more to life than the pursuit of pleasure.

Siddhartha began travelling beyond his palace. What he experienced deeply shocked him.

- On his first journey he met an old man and learned about *old age.*
- On his second journey he met a man covered in sores and learned about *illness.*
- On his third journey he saw a corpse about to be cremated and learned about *death.*
- On his fourth journey he met a wandering ascetic who wore a simple yellow robe and had only a few possessions. From him he learned that *true*

happiness cannot be achieved either by amassing great wealth or by the pursuit of pleasure.

These four experiences, which profoundly changed Siddhartha's whole outlook on life, are called the *Four Sights*.

Siddhartha decided to devote the rest of his life to finding answers to life's great mysteries.

On the *Blessed Night of the Great Renunciation* he rejected his royal status by taking on the identity of a beggar, and left his family, never to return.

For the next five years, Siddhartha lived as a wandering ascetic. As he had been raised a Hindu he sought answers in the Vedas (Hindu scriptures) and from various *gurus* (teachers). However, since neither could provide him with the answers he sought, he decided to reject Hinduism and find answers by his own efforts.

On Siddhartha's thirty-fifth birthday there occurred what Buddhists call the *Sacred Night*. He sat beneath a banyan tree (known since as the *Bo Tree* or *Tree of Wisdom*) and meditated on all that he had experienced and learned. After three nights he gained *enlightenment*: a deep understanding of the meaning of life. He then travelled to Benares, where he began preaching his message and made many converts. His followers gave him the title *Buddha* (or *Enlightened One*). By the time of his death forty-four years later, Buddhism was firmly established, and soon spread throughout south-east Asia.

SACRED TEXT

TABLE 5.1

Title	The *Pali Canon* *Pali* is an ancient northern Indian language, which may have been spoken by the Buddha. *Canon* means an agreed set of writings.
Date	Written in the first century B.C. by Buddhist monks and nuns in Sri Lanka. They recorded the stories and sayings of the Buddha, which had been passed on orally for several centuries.

BUDDHISM 73

TABLE 5.1 (contd.)

Content	Consists of forty-five volumes divided into three sections known as the *Tripitaka* (the *Three Baskets*): • the *Vinaya* (Discipline Basket), which contains the rules for the *Sangha* (Buddhist community of monks and nuns) • the *Sutta* (Instruction Basket), which contains Buddha's sermons • the *Abhimdhamma* (Great Teaching Basket), which contains analyses of Buddha's most profound and important teachings.

BELIEFS

Karma

Everything is subject to the *law of Karma* (the law of actions and their effects). This states:

From good must come good, from evil must come evil.

Everything a person thinks, says and does has an impact in this or a future life:

- if a person does something good it creates *positive* karma.
- if a person does something bad it creates *negative* karma.

Reincarnation

Human beings must undergo *reincarnation* – a long cycle of birth, death and rebirth – until they finally accumulate enough positive karma to free themselves by achieving *nirvana*, i.e. the state of complete happiness and perfect peace.

The Four Noble Truths

People can only achieve nirvana by accepting the four noble truths:

1 all life is *dukkha* (suffering)
2 dukkha is caused by *desire* (wanting things)

3 dukkha can only be overcome by ceasing to desire
4 this can only be achieved by following the *eightfold path*.

The Eightfold Path

These are the eight steps one must follow to end dukkha and achieve nirvana:

1 right views – be positive in outlook
2 right thoughts – care for others
3 right speech – speak well of others where possible
4 right action – help others in practical ways
5 right livelihood – do worthwhile work
6 right effort – work hard, be a committed person
7 right mindfulness – be attentive in thought and action
8 right concentration – be at peace with oneself and the world.

DIVISIONS

(Higher Level only)

After the Buddha's death, two distinct strands emerged in Buddhism: *Theravada* and *Mahayana*.

Theravada (*the way of the elders*) is the oldest school of Buddhist thought. Its followers believe that:

- the Buddha was a great and holy man, but *not* a god
- the only authentic source of guidance on how to achieve nirvana is to be found in the Pali Canon.

Mahayana means *the great vehicle*. Most of the world's Buddhists belong to this group. Its members (influenced by Hinduism) believe that:

- the Buddha was a god (and they conduct elaborate rituals to worship him)
- there are *Bodhisattvas* – people who have already achieved enlightenment but chose to remain on earth to help others achieve nirvana.

Despite these differences, both strands of Buddhism agree that:

BUDDHISM

- any person can achieve nirvana by faithfully following the Buddha's teachings
- Siddhartha Gautama was not the only Buddha: there have been many others in human history. For example, Tibetan Buddhists believe that their leader, known as the *Dalai Lama* (which means *guru as great as the ocean*) is the reincarnation of the Buddha.

BUDDHISM TODAY

(Higher Level only)

Worldwide

Buddhism is the world's fourth largest religion. Estimates of its membership vary from 350 to 400 million worldwide.

Buddhism is the majority religion in Sri Lanka and the state religion of Bhutan and Thailand. There are substantial Buddhist populations in the other nations of South East Asia.

In recent times Buddhism has gained many new converts in China (since the death of Chairman Mao) and in India (among the Untouchables).

Ireland

Buddhism has spread outside South East Asia and has begun to attract a small but growing number of members in Western Europe and North America.

The first Buddhist centre in Ireland, Kagyu Samye Dzong, was established in 1977 at Kilmainham, Dublin. Another, Dzogchen Beara Retreat Centre, was later set up in West Cork. Both offer instruction in meditation and the Buddhist way of life.

Section D

6 The Question of Faith

THE SITUATION OF FAITH TODAY

Meaning

Faith involves:

- belief in God
- love of God
- belief in what God has revealed (as recorded in the sacred texts of one's religion)
- trust in God's goodness.

Role of Faith

A *community of faith* exists where people have a religion in common, i.e. they share the same set of beliefs and worship in the same way.

Devout (dedicated) members of a particular religion claim that their faith is *central* to their whole way of life because it:

- inspires them to live better lives
- gives them the strength needed to face life's many challenges.
- offers them hope for life beyond the grave.

Religion plays an important role in human affairs. Indeed, like art and technology, religion is one of the things that sets human beings apart from all other creatures on this planet.

THE BEGINNINGS OF FAITH

Origins of Religion

The precise date when religion began is uncertain. However, excavations at the Border Cave in South Africa indicate that people may have had some form of religious beliefs as early as eighty thousand years ago.

Religion most likely began as an attempt by early humans to understand and explain the workings of their environment, e.g. why the weather changed. At first people believed that the different aspects of nature (the sun, wind, rain etc.) were some kinds of higher powers or gods.

Later, they stopped believing that the different aspects of nature were gods and began to believe that there were invisible gods who controlled the elements: the rainfall, the heat of the sun and so on.

Our ancestors believed that the behaviour of these gods depended on their mood; and if they were angry they would punish people. As a result, people believed that they had to please the gods by making sacrifices to them, e.g. offering them the lives of animals.

In time the five major religions emerged.

TABLE 6.1

Name	Date of emergence	Percentage of world's population*
Hinduism	2000 B.C.	13.5
Judaism	1850 B.C.	0.3
Buddhism	500 B.C.	5.5
Christianity	4 B.C.	34
Islam	A.D. 622	20

*as of 2005

Kinds of Religion

- *Monotheism* means belief in one god only.
- *Polytheism* means belief in more than one god.

Judaism, Christianity and Islam are all monotheistic religions.

Mystery and Religion

Human beings are faced with two different kinds of question:

- *Problems*, e.g. How can a disease be cured? How can a security code be broken? Given sufficient time, resources and know-how, these questions can be fully answered by human beings
- *Mysteries*, e.g. Why do bad things happen to good people? How can people find true happiness? Such questions *cannot* be fully answered by human beings. This is where religion comes in. Each of the major religions seeks, in its own way, to help people to gain insights into life's mysteries and grow in their understanding of them.

The Existence of God

There are three possible responses to the question 'Does God exist?' They are:

- *theism* – yes, there is a God
- *atheism* – no, there is no God
- *agnosticism* – don't know; it is impossible to answer this question one way or the other.

Reasons for Belief in God

The Jewish, Christian and Muslim religions teach that God is a *pure spirit*. In other words, God does not have a physical body.

While they admit there is no direct evidence that God exists they claim that there is *indirect* evidence to support belief in God.

Consider the following:

- *the existence of the world.* The world did not just simply come into existence by itself. Things only happen because something else *makes* them happen. The world was created by God
- *the evidence of order and design in the world.* Consider all the factors that make life possible on earth, such as the delicate balance of gases or its position relative to the sun. This did not happen by accident. The world was designed and ordered in this way by God.

THE GROWTH OF FAITH

The Stages of Faith

This is only a general outline of the development of a person's faith.

Stage 1: Childhood Faith (birth to 12 years)
Young children tend to believe what they are told by adults they trust. The example of parents/guardians and older siblings is very important: they help children to develop their religious identity and sense of self-worth. At this stage children learn and come to understand the stories, beliefs and practices of their particular religion.

Stage 2: Adolescent Faith (13 to 18 years)
Young people begin to wonder about life and question what they have been told. They strive to develop their own understanding of their religion and what it demands of them. This may lead to a strengthening of their faith or to a partial or even complete rejection of it.

At this stage their families' commitment to living out the teachings of their particular religion is vitally important as it offers support and encouragement at a confusing time in their lives.

Stage 3: Mature Faith (19 years and over)
At this stage people should:

- have worked out what they believe and value and why they do so
- be committed and strive to live according to their faith
- be confident about their own beliefs and be respectful of those whose beliefs differ from their own.

Influences on the Development of Faith

Factors that influence the development of a person's faith include:

- *home* – through the education and example given by parents/guardians
- *parish* – through involvement in religious rituals and social activities that reinforce one's beliefs

THE QUESTION OF FAITH

- *school* – through religious instruction and the example set by the teaching personnel.

Images of God

As a person's faith matures, his/her image of God should undergo important changes.

A child might imagine God in the following ways:

- as a nice old man with a beard who sits on a throne in the clouds
- as someone who is only interested in catching people out if they do something wrong
- as a shoulder to cry on when things go wrong but someone you ignore the rest of the time.

Some people continue to see God in this way even in adulthood. However, a person of mature faith is one who realises that God is none of these things. God is the greatest mystery of all.

Judaism, Christianity and Islam teach that God loves each and every human being. God is always there to guide people, in good times and in bad.

God in the World's Religions

Hinduism

- Hindus are free to worship different gods.
- The most prominent Hindu gods are *Brahma* (the Creator), *Vishnu* (the Preserver) and *Shiva* (the Destroyer).
- All the different gods and the entire universe itself are expressions of something greater – *Brahman* (the World Soul).
- Brahman is the impersonal source of all things and the energy that sustains all things.
- The goal of human life is to achieve *nirvana*, i.e. to be absorbed into Brahman after death.

Buddhism

- According to the Theravada tradition, the Buddha was a holy man who rejected belief in a god or gods.

- According to the Mahayana tradition, the Buddha was a god. There are elaborate systems for worshipping him.

Judaism, Christianity and Islam are all monotheistic religions. They agree that God is the loving, just and all-powerful creator and sustainer of the universe.

Judaism

- God's name is *Yahweh*.
- However, God's name is too holy to be spoken. Instead, out of deep respect, Jews refer to God as *Adonai* (meaning *the Lord*).

Islam

- The Shahadah states, 'There is no God but Allah and Muhammad is his prophet.'
- Muslims believe that the Qur'an is *literally* the word of God.

Christianity

There are two key Christian teachings about God – the *Incarnation* and the *Trinity*. Both are complex and easily misunderstood.

The Incarnation

- Christians believe that in Jesus of Nazareth, God became a human being and that Jesus is *God made man*.
- This does *not* mean that Jesus is part God and part human.
- It does mean that Jesus is both fully God and fully human. He is *true God and true man* (Catechism of the Catholic Church).

The Trinity

- Jesus constantly referred to God as his Father. Jesus's disciples came to believe that he was the *Son of God*.
- Jesus promised to send the *Holy Spirit* after his ascension. This happened at Pentecost.
- Christians began to pray to *God the Father, God the Son and God the Holy Spirit*.

THE QUESTION OF FAITH

- The Apostles' Creed sets out the doctrine (teaching) of the *Trinity*.

Christians worship only one God, but they believe that there are three distinct persons in the one God.

St Patrick is said to have used the shamrock to help people understand the doctrine of the Trinity. The shamrock has three leaves but is one plant. The Trinity has three persons but there is only one God. Each person reveals God relating to the world in a different way.

THE EXPRESSION OF FAITH

In this section we look at the life stories of two faithful people from different religious traditions.

Mohandas K. Gandhi – Hindu Tradition

- Born in India in 1869. Educated at the University of London. A lawyer by profession.
- Was involved in opposing the racist policies of the South African government for twenty years until his return to India in 1915.
- Achieved great renown as a Hindu holy man and religious teacher. Popularly referred to as the *Mahatma* (the *Great Soul*).
- Became leader of the Indian National Congress in 1920. Led its campaign to achieve India's independence from the British Empire.
- Developed *satyagraha* (meaning *steadfastness in truth*), which consisted of the theory and practice of non-violent resistance.

- Believed that refusing to retaliate violently would eventually defeat an opponent, though it would demand great sacrifice and suffering.
- Led protest marches against unjust British policies and organised boycotts of British goods.
- Was imprisoned on many occasions by the British authorities.
- Credited as the architect of Indian independence when it was achieved in 1947.
- Assassinated by a Hindu extremist on 30 January 1948.

Mother Teresa – Christian Tradition

- Born in Yugoslavia in 1910.
- Decided to become a Catholic nun.
- Trained by Mercy Sisters in Rathfarnham, Dublin.
- Became a secondary school principal in Calcutta.
- Referred to 10 September 1946 as her 'Day of Decision'. Asked permission of her superiors to work with the poor in the slums of Calcutta.
- Was given permission to do so. Trained to be a nurse and returned to Calcutta in 1948.
- Established a new religious order, the Missionaries of Charity, with the Pope's approval in 1950. All sisters wear white saris edged with blue stripes. In addition to vows of poverty, chastity and obedience, they take an extra vow of pledging service to the poor.
- Opened first home for the dying in 1952. Expanded services as the order increased in size. Set up hospitals to care for lepers, and schools for slum children.
- Was awarded *Padmashri* (*Lord of the Lotus*) by the Indian government for her work with the poor.
- Was awarded the Nobel Peace Prize in 1979.
- Died in 1997. Was mourned by countless millions. Her religious order now cares for the poor in over 200 centres worldwide.

CHALLENGES TO FAITH

(Higher Level only)

Religion and Science

Science is a term that refers to any area of study in which knowledge is acquired by observation, experiment and reasoning.

Technology concerns the practical application of scientific discoveries to everyday life.

Origins of the Conflict between Religion and Science

The condemnation of the Italian astronomer Galileo Galilei (1564–1642) did much to encourage the view that religion is opposed to science and that science is the enemy of religion.

Until the seventeenth century, most people accepted Aristotle's model of the universe with the earth stationary at the centre and the sun and other planets rotating around it.

By that time, however, the work of Copernicus and Kepler had led some people to doubt this model.

Galileo built on their work and used the newly invented telescope to observe the movements of the planets. This led him to conclude that Aristotle's model was wrong, and that the earth goes round the sun and not the other way round.

The Catholic Church authorities had taught for centuries that the earth was the centre of the universe. They feared that people's confidence in the Church as a source of guidance would be shattered. As a result, they over-reacted:

- they banned the study of Copernicus' and Kepler's work.
- Galileo was ordered to say that his discovery was only a hypothesis (possible explanation) and that it could not be proved.

At first Galileo agreed to do this. Later he changed his mind and in 1632 he published his findings.

The Catholic Church authorities put him on trial for contradicting them. Under threat of torture, Galileo was forced to recant (take back what he had said). Galileo was kept under house arrest for the rest of his life.

Although this event happened centuries ago and the Catholic Church has since apologised, it has left a lasting mark on the way in which people see the relationship between religion and science. It has encouraged the view that religion and science are at best rivals and at worst enemies.

The Question of Creation

Until the mid-nineteenth century, most Christians thought that what they read in the book of Genesis about the creation of the universe was literally true, i.e. that the world was made by God in six days.

In 1656 the Protestant archbishop James Ussher claimed that the creation began on 23 October 4004 B.C.

Scientists studying the fossilised remains of long-extinct creatures (e.g. dinosaurs) concluded that the earth was far older. Eventually it was discovered that the universe began over 18 billion years ago and that the earth was formed about 4.5 billion years ago.

The most influential scientist working in this field was Charles Darwin. He presented his ideas in two books: *On the Origin of Species* (1859) and *The Descent of Man* (1871).

Darwin put forward the *theory of evolution*, which said that all life (including humans) had evolved over millions of years by the process of natural selection.

His work challenged the literal reading of Genesis. Most leading churchmen rejected it at first. However, as later scientists revised certain aspects of Darwin's work, many Christians came to accept some form of the theory of evolution.

In time many Christians concluded that the Genesis account of creation was *inspired* by God but not dictated by God. It was never intended to be a literal explanation of the creation. Rather, it was a poetic account intended to convey important religious teachings:

- God created the world from nothing
- God's creation is good
- God created human beings
- God has given human beings a special place in and responsibility for creation.

Many Christians today believe that Genesis and Darwin need not cause conflict between religion and science, because the theory of evolution explains *how* life began and the Genesis account explains *why* life began. Religion and science each tackles a different question.

The Relationship between Religion and Science
We can identify two approaches.
Conflict: religion and science offer two opposing systems of belief. A person must accept one and reject the other.
Partnership: religion and science need each other. Each answers important questions – religion asks 'why'; science asks 'how'. Each adds something to our understanding of life. They complement each other. They are partners in the search for truth.

CHALLENGES TO RELIGIOUS EXPERIENCE

(Higher Level only)

Secularism

Secularism refers to the *decline in active membership of organised religion and the lessening of religious influence on people's values.*

Secularism is largely a western European phenomenon: religion is on the increase elsewhere. Despite the growth of secularism, however, the majority of Europeans still believe in God and in life after death.

Although there has been a decline in the number of Irish Catholics attending weekly mass, certain expectations persist. For example, even those who identify themselves as no longer formally members of a particular religion expect to be able to:

- marry in a church
- have their children christened there
- hold funeral services in a church.

There still persists a sense that religion has an important role to play in people's lives.

Humanism

Humanism is a term often used to refer to all those alternatives to traditional organised religion.

Humanists consider the growth of secularism to be a positive development because they believe that religion has been and continues to act as a barrier to human progress.

Humanists are either atheists or agnostics. They neither believe in God nor see any need for God. They believe that people can be happy and fulfilled without any religious dimension to their lives. Humanists consider morality to be a code for living that has been invented entirely by human beings. They argue that issues of right and wrong can be decided by human reason alone, without any reference to God.

Religious people profoundly disagree with the humanist outlook. They claim that:

- religion is a necessary and trustworthy guide to living a good life
- religion has and continues to be a great force for good and vital source of hope in people's lives.

Section E

7 The Celebration of Faith

PRAYER

Meaning

Prayer has been described as a *conversation from the heart between God and human beings.*
Prayer consists of two elements:

- giving thanks and praise *to* God
- seeking help and forgiveness *from* God.

Importance

Prayer is vitally important for building and sustaining a strong and lasting relationship with God.

Methods

Prayer can be either *vocal* or *silent*.

Vocal
Vocal prayer can be:

- *formal* – with a fixed format that has been taken from a religion's sacred text (e.g. the Our Father from the New Testament)
- *informal* – composed by a believer him/herself.

People might also sing a hymn or play a piece of instrumental music.

Silent
Silent prayer is also known as *meditation*. It requires self-discipline, practice and patience. The stages involved in meditation include:

- calming one's body by consciously relaxing the muscles and breathing deeply and rhythmically to achieve an inner quiet
- then focusing one's attention on God by reading and reflecting on a passage from a sacred text and trying to see how its message can be applied to one's daily life.

The highest form of meditation is *contemplation*. It involves no words at all, just the sense of being in union with God.

Analysis of a Formal Prayer

Example: the Lord's Prayer or the Our Father.
(see *Matthew* 6:7–16)

TABLE 7.1

Prayer	Explanation
1. Our Father, who art in heaven,	God is the Father, i.e. loving parent, of all people and he invites all people to share eternal life with him.
2. hallowed be thy name.	God's name is to be respected.
3. Thy kingdom come. Thy will be done on earth, as it is in heaven.	People should work with God to bring his plan for creation to fulfilment.
4. Give us this day our daily bread,	God will provide us with what we need.
5. and forgive us our trespasses, as we forgive those who trespass against us,	Being forgiven by God depends on forgiving those who have offended us.
6. and lead us not into temptation, but deliver us from evil.	God is to be trusted. God will strengthen people in times of crisis or temptation.

THE CELEBRATION OF FAITH

Reasons for Prayer

People usually turn to God in prayer for one or more of the following reasons:

- they are deeply shaken by an experience of suffering
- they are sorry for some wrong they have inflicted on others
- they are grateful when something important works out
- they are overjoyed at having the love of another person
- they are awed by an experience of the beauty and power of nature
- they realise how short and swiftly ended life can be.

Types of Prayer

There are six types of prayer:

- *adoration*: a sense of mystery and wonder
- *intercession*: love for other people and a wish to help them
- *petition*: an awareness of one's own needs
- *contrition*: a realisation of where one has gone wrong in one's life and a desire to live a better life
- *protection*: a sense of the power of evil and an awareness of the suffering it causes
- *thanksgiving*: a deep gratitude to God for all those people and things that are important to oneself.

Experience of Prayer

Judaism

Devout Jews follow the example set for them by the patriarchs and pray three times each day:

- *in the morning*: because Abraham prayed early in the morning
- *in the afternoon*: because Isaac stopped his work to pray in the afternoon
- *in the evening*: because Jacob thanked God in the evening.

They do this to demonstrate and strengthen their commitment to keeping the covenant that God made with their ancestors.

Islam

According to the Qur'an, a practising Muslim must pray five times each day — at dawn, noon, mid-afternoon, sunset and evening.

In Muslim countries, the muezzin calls the faithful to prayer. Attendance at Friday prayers is compulsory. Men and women worship separately.

On arrival at the mosque, Muslims remove their shoes, put on skullcaps and perform *wudu* (ritual washing) to prepare their minds and bodies. Kneeling on mats, they face in the direction of Makkah.

After the imam's sermon, they recite prayers according to a set format, each gesture saying something about a Muslim's relationship with Allah. For example:

- *standing*: to show alertness to the words of Allah
- *bowing*: to demonstrate love and respect for Allah
- *prostration*: to show surrender to Allah
- *sitting*: to indicate tranquillity and acceptance of the will of Allah.

THE EXPERIENCE OF WORSHIP

Meaning

Worship involves *any action by which people show that they recognise the supreme importance of God as the creator and sustainer of the universe.*

Sense of the Sacred

Worship springs forth from the *sense of the sacred*. This refers to people's *awareness of the invisible and mysterious presence of God in their lives*. This sense of the sacred is expressed in symbols and celebrated in rituals.

Ritual

A ritual is a *formal religious ceremony, approved by religious authorities, which gives a regular pattern to people's worship of God.*

Examples

The sacraments are public rituals. The word *sacrament* means a *holy mystery*. Catholic and Orthodox Christians believe that there are seven sacraments:

THE CELEBRATION OF FAITH

- baptism
- confirmation
- eucharist
- reconciliation
- matrimony
- holy orders
- anointing the sick.

In these sacraments Christians recall and re-enact the life, death and resurrection of Jesus Christ. In each one, they celebrate the presence of Jesus in the key moments of people's lives.

TABLE 7.2

Baptism	birth
Confirmation	growth to maturity
Eucharist	living and sharing with others
Reconciliation	failure and forgiveness
Matrimony	marriage
Holy orders	sacred ministry
Anointing	illness, healing and death

Sign and Symbol

Sign and symbol must be carefully distinguished from each other.

A *sign* is a concrete image, word or gesture that points beyond itself, but has only one fixed, clear and unambiguous meaning. For example, a red light at a road junction is a simple sign that means 'stop'.

A *symbol* is also a concrete image, word or gesture that points beyond itself, but it has *more* than one meaning.

A symbol has a much richer content than a sign. It enables people to express ideas that are very difficult to put into words.

Symbols play an important role in religion. They can help people to be more aware of and focus their minds on the invisible presence of God in their lives.

TABLE 7.3 The Symbols of the Major Religions

Religion	Symbol	Explanation
Judaism		The menorah, a seven-branched candlestick, stood in the Temple in Jerusalem in ancient times and its design is described in the Torah. The central branch is said to represent the Sabbath, the day on which God rested after creating the world.
Christianity		Jesus died on the cross, the normal method of execution in the Roman Empire at that time. It was a shameful and painful death, but Christians believe that by dying in this way Jesus showed his power over sin, suffering and death.
Islam		Muslims say that Islam guides a person's life just as the moon and stars guide a traveller at night in the desert. This symbol on a country's flag often indicates that it is a Muslim state.
Hinduism		This is the written form of the sacred sound 'Aum' (sometimes spelled 'Om'). According to the sacred Hindu texts, Aum was the first sound, out of which the rest of the universe was created.
Buddhism		The Buddha spoke of an Eightfold Path to enlightenment. This is traditionally represented as an eight-spoked wheel. The path is a guide to living life compassionately and non-violently.

THE CELEBRATION OF FAITH

Christian Symbols
Cross/crucifix

The cross is almost always found in Christian places of worship.

Jesus died on the cross. Christians believe that through his death and resurrection God showed his power over sin, suffering and death. A *crucifix* is a cross with a figure of Jesus hanging from it.

The fish

Perhaps the most popular symbol among early Christians was the fish. The Greek word for fish is *ichthys*. Each letter of the word points to a name or title for Jesus.

TABLE 7.4

I	Iesos	Jesus	Meaning:
Ch	Christos	Christ	*Jesus Christ, God's Son, Saviour*
Th	Theou	Of God	
Y	Yios	Son	
S	Soter	Saviour	

Icon

The word *icon* comes from the Greek word meaning *image*.

An icon is a richly decorated painting of Jesus, Mary, a saint or an angel or a combination of these religious figures.

Every detail in an icon is intended to convey an important religious idea. Consider the *Teaching Christ* (sixteenth century, Moscow school) pictured left.

This is an icon of Jesus. The doctrine of the incarnation teaches that Jesus is true God and true man. Gold and blue colours are used to suggest the belief that

Jesus is *divine*.

The *humanity* of Jesus is suggested by the brown, earthy colour that was used for the inner garment.

Icons are widely used by Christians in the *Orthodox* tradition to help them focus their minds on the mystery of God.

Ashes on Ash Wednesday

Ash Wednesday is the first day of Lent. Catholics attend mass and their foreheads are marked with ashes. This is done to remind them that, though following Jesus involves suffering, the way of the cross leads to new life, to resurrection and eternal life with God.

Jewish Symbols

Yarmulke

This is a skullcap worn by Jewish men. It is worn to demonstrate respect for God. It reminds Jews that God's wisdom is vastly greater than that of human beings. While there is no religious rule requiring Jewish males to wear the yarmulke, most do so because they believe that praying bareheaded shows serious disrespect to God.

Tefillen

These are two cube-shaped leather boxes, each of which contains four passages from the Tenakh.

One box is strapped to a Jewish man's forehead to remind him to *think* about what his religion teaches. The other box is tied around his upper forearm next to his heart to remind him to *act* on what his religion teaches.

THE CELEBRATION OF FAITH

Tallit

This is a prayer shawl made of silk or wool. It is usually coloured blue and white and has fringes attached to its four corners as laid down in *Numbers* 15:37–41. The tallit is worn, draped across a man's shoulders, at morning prayers only.

Mezuzah

Jews consider the home to be a sacred place. The most visible symbol of this is the mezuzah. It is a small decorated container, which is fixed to the upper third of all doorposts in a Jewish home, except for the doors to the toilet, bathroom and garage.

The mezuzah contains the verses of the *Shema* (*Deuteronomy* 6:4–9).

Jews touch the mezuzah when entering or leaving a room to show their love for God and to remind themselves of their Jewish beliefs and identity.

Buddhist Symbols

Buddhists believe that:

- *light* symbolises the wisdom that drives away the darkness caused by ignorance and prejudice
- *incense* gives off a beautiful fragrance that symbolises the moral purity that each person should strive to achieve
- *flowers* are a reminder that all things pass away and that people should not pointlessly strive to fill their lives with material possessions.

Examples of Worship

Judaism – Shabbat

According to the Torah, God commanded that the seventh day of the week should be a day of worship and relaxation.

Jews refer to the seventh day as Shabbat or the Sabbath day. It begins at sunset on Friday and runs through until nightfall on Saturday.

Many devout Jews believe that all business activities, shopping, housework and the use of most technology should be avoided on the Sabbath day.

Jews may attend a service in the synagogue on Saturday morning or on the previous Friday evening. The service consists of:

- readings from the Torah
- prayers and hymns
- a sermon on the readings.

Faithful observance of the Shabbat is considered vitally important as it encourages Jews to keep the covenant God made with their ancestors.

Catholicism – the Mass

The mass is also known as the sacrament of the eucharist.

The word *eucharist* means *thanksgiving*.

The mass is the focal point of the *liturgy* (i.e. public rituals) of the Catholic Church. It has its origins in the words and actions of Jesus at the Last Supper.

Only a Catholic bishop or priest is allowed to lead the congregation in worship at a mass.

Only a Catholic bishop or priest can *consecrate* the bread and wine so that it becomes the body and blood of Jesus (see *Worship as a Response to Mystery*, page 118).

However, the mass is a communal act, as all those present are gathered in Christ's name to share in celebrating the *Paschal Mystery* (i.e., his death and resurrection).

Catholics believe that Jesus is *really present* in the mass, just as he was to the disciples two thousand years ago. The participants in the mass encounter him in three ways:

- in the sacred texts
- in the breaking of bread
- in their fellow human beings.

The basic elements and overall structure of the mass was settled by the second century A.D. Its four sections are:

THE CELEBRATION OF FAITH

1 Introductory Rites (including the Penitential Rite)
2 Liturgy of the Word
3 Liturgy of the Eucharist
4 Concluding Rites.

When Catholics receive the Eucharist at Holy Communion they undertake to put Jesus's teaching into practice in their daily lives.

THE WORLD OF RITUAL

Places of Worship

Christianity – the Church

A Non-conformist Church

An Orthodox Church

A church is a building specifically designed and used by Christians for the worship of God.

The earliest Christian churches date from the fourth century A.D., when the Emperor Constantine granted them freedom of worship. Before then, Christians had been persecuted and had to worship in secret places.

There are significant differences in the architecture and decoration of churches in the different Christian traditions.

Non-conformist Christians (e.g. Presbyterians) worship in simply designed buildings that are plainly decorated.

The pulpit is the focal point of the building because non-conformist worship emphasises listening to the Word of God.

Catholic and *Orthodox* churches are more ornate, with paintings, statues, stained-glass windows and shrines.

Although the pulpit is important,

A Catholic Church

the altar is the focal point in these buildings. However, *Orthodox* churches differ from Catholic ones by having few seats (most worshippers are expected to stand) and a feature called an *iconostasis*.

This is a screen, decorated with pictures, that separates the main part of the church from the *sanctuary* (the altar area).

Judaism – the Synagogue

The word synagogue comes from the Greek word *synagein*, meaning *to gather together*.

A synagogue is a simple rectangular building, which serves three purposes:

- a *house of prayer* where services are held each Sabbath and festival day
- a *place of education* where children learn Hebrew and study the Tenakh
- a *community centre* for meetings of various Jewish organisations.

The synagogue became the centre of Jewish community life after the destruction of the Temple in A.D. 70 and the dispersion of the Jewish people out of Palestine in A.D. 135.

Some features of the synagogue recall aspects of the Temple:

- its layout is based on that of the Temple
- it faces towards Jerusalem, where the Temple once stood.

In traditional synagogues, men and women sit separately.

Key features of a synagogue are shown in the diagram on following page.

1 *Ner Tamid* (Perpetual Lamp). Hangs above and before the *Ark*. Represents the menorah (seven-branched candlestick), which was always lit in the Temple.
2 *Aron Hakodesh* (the Ark). This is a special alcove/cupboard set into the wall facing Jerusalem. Contains *Sefer Torah*.
3 *Sefer Torah*. Sacred text hand-written on parchment scrolls.
4 *Bimah*. Reading desk on raised platform where the rabbi gives the sermon and the Torah is read. Seating is arranged around it.

THE CELEBRATION OF FAITH

5 *Memorial.* Lists names of the deceased members of the Jewish community.
6 *Magen David.* The Star of David – symbol of Jerusalem.

Islam – the Mosque

The name means the *place of prostration*.
A mosque serves two functions:

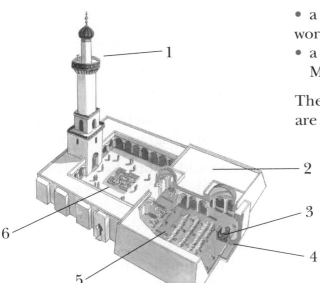

- a place where Allah is worshipped
- a centre for the education of Muslim children.

The key features of a mosque are indicated in the diagram.

1 *Minaret.* The tower from which the muezzin (crier) calls Muslims to prayer. Attendance on Friday is compulsory.
2 *Women's area.* Usually an enclosed gallery. Men and women pray in separate areas.
3 *Minbar.* A raised platform from which the imam gives the sermon and leads prayers.
4 *Mihrab.* An alcove in a wall that points towards Makkah.
5 *Communal prayer.* Everyone sits in rows on the floor to emphasise the belief that everyone is equal before Allah.
6 *Wudu area.* This is where ritual washing is carried out before worship begins.

Mosques are decorated only with calligraphy and geometric designs. The Qur'an forbids the drawing or painting of any image of Allah. Any attempt to do so is *shirk* (blasphemy).

Hinduism – the Mandir (Temple)

Hindu *puja* (acts of worship) take place both in the home and in the mandir. Food and flowers are offered as an expression of devotion to the gods.

The mandir serves as both a place of worship and a community meeting place.

The key features of a mandir are indicated in the diagram.

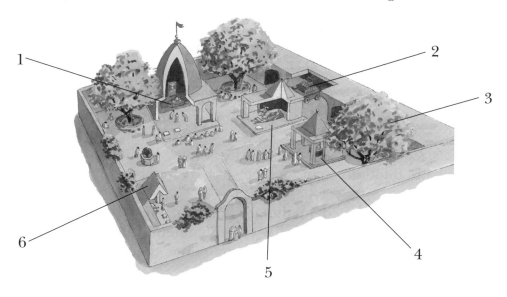

THE CELEBRATION OF FAITH

1 *Primary shrine.* Only the priests may enter the shrine room. They awaken, bathe, dress, feed and put the statue of the god to sleep.
2 *Rath.* A ceremonial chariot used to process the statue of the god at festival times.
3 *Trees.* They are honoured because they give life and offer shelter.
4 *Secondary shrine.* If the temple is dedicated to Vishnu, this will be for Shiva, and vice versa.
5 *Nandi.* Figure of the bull. Revered in Hindu culture for his strength. Usually found alongside shrines to Shiva.
6 *Memorial shrine.* This is dedicated to deceased local holy men. (Their bodies are usually cremated and the ashes scattered in the River Ganges.)

Buddhism – the Temple

A Buddhist temple is usually a part of a *sangha*, a monastery where Buddhist monks and nuns live as a community.

The key features of a temple are indicated in the diagram.

1 *Temple complex.* This consists of a shrine room, meditation rooms and teaching halls. Buddhists remove their shoes before entering as a mark of respect.
2 *Statue of Buddha.* Situated in the shrine room. Shown sitting in lotus (meditation) position to symbolise enlightenment. Buddhists recite the three refuges, bow three times before the statue, then burn candles and incense to create positive karma.

3 *Bell* and 4 *Drum*. The bell is rung and the drum beaten during festival times. Smaller bells inside the shrine room are rung during daily devotions.

Times of Significance

All the major religions have rituals that mark significant moments in the lives of their members.

Birth

Christianity — the sacrament of baptism

The word *baptism* comes from the Greek word *baptizo*, which means *to dip*.

Baptism may be received only once. It is a ritual of naming, welcoming and thanksgiving.

The elements of the ceremony are as follows.

- The parents present the child for baptism and are welcomed by the priest.
- Also present are the godparents, who promise to help in bringing up the child as a Christian.
- The child is anointed twice, with *oil of catechumens* (symbolising the strength that comes from God's grace); and *oil of chrism* (symbolising the call to live by God's standards).
- The parents and godparents renew their own baptismal vows and commit themselves to educate the child in the Christian faith.
- Water is poured over the child's head to symbolise the purifying power of the Holy Spirit. Then the child is formally named.
- A white shawl is wrapped around the child as a symbol that he/she shares in the resurrection of Jesus.
- A candle is lit to remind all present that Jesus's resurrection is their guarantee that death is not the end but a gateway to eternal life with God.
- The priest blesses the child to remind those present that the child belongs to and is a gift from God.

Islam — Aqiqa

Aqiqa is the Muslim naming ceremony.

THE CELEBRATION OF FAITH

The birth of a child is regarded as *barakah*: a blessing from Allah. The child's father whispers the *adhan* (muezzin's call to prayer) into the child's right ear after his/her birth.

Seven days after the birth the ritual of Aqiqa is held.

- The child's head is shaved and its weight in gold or silver is given to the poor.
- The parents make a sacrifice to give thanks for the child – two sheep if it is a boy and one sheep if it is a girl. One-third of the sacrifice is given to the poor.
- The child is named, either after Muhammad or one of his family, or with a name that has a religious meaning (e.g. Abdullah, which means Servant of Allah).
- Boys are usually circumcised, although this sometimes occurs in a separate ceremony at the age of seven.

Judaism – naming and circumcision

Children are considered a blessing and gift from God (*Psalm* 127).

Boys. Eight days after a boy is born, he is formally named at a ceremony held in the local synagogue. The name chosen has a meaning, e.g. Isaiah (God is salvation); Joshua (Saviour). On the same day the ritual of *Brit Milah* (the covenant of the circumcision) takes place.

Circumcision involves the removal of the loose foreskin over the penis. This operation is carried out by a *mohel* (a man specially trained for this task).

Circumcision is taught to be necessary for all male Jews because it is believed to have been demanded by God when he made his covenant with Abraham (see *Genesis* 17:9–14).

Girls. A Jewish girl is usually given her name on the first Sabbath (Saturday) after her birth.

In reformed and liberal Jewish communities, a girl is given her name when she is seven days old in a ceremony called *Zeved Habat* (which means 'gift of a daughter').

Adulthood

Christianity – the sacrament of confirmation

Confirmation comes from the Latin word *confirmare*, meaning to strengthen. Confirmation is a sacrament of initiation and may be received only once. It strengthens baptised Christians and through the power of the Holy Spirit helps them to be active and committed followers of Christ.

Since the Middle Ages the Catholic Church has offered the sacrament of confirmation to young Catholics entering their teenage years. However, the Orthodox Church continues the earlier practice of baptising and confirming in the same ceremony.

The ceremony in the Catholic Church consists of the following elements.

- The renewal of baptismal vows: the young person is thought to be ready to make these on his/her own.
- The stretching out of hands: the bishop asks for God's grace to strengthen a person to fulfil his/her vocation (calling).
- Anointing with chrism: this symbolises the power of the Holy Spirit strengthening the young person in his/her commitment to following Christ.

Judaism – Bar Mitzvah and Bat Mitzvah

Boys are declared adults at the age of thirteen. The *Bar Mitzvah* (Son of the Commandments) is a ceremony held to mark a boy's new status as an adult. Judaism recognises that girls generally mature earlier than boys, and girls are considered adults at the age of twelve. The *Bat Mitzvah* (Daughter of the Commandments) is a ceremony held by Jews in reformed and liberal communities to mark a girl's new status as an adult.

Both boys and girls spend several years preparing for the relevant ceremony. They must learn Hebrew so they can read from the Torah in the synagogue. A celebratory meal is held after the ceremony.

In these ceremonies young Jews commit themselves to living out their beliefs faithfully in their daily lives.

KEY FESTIVALS

The Calendar

The religious calendar marks the passage of time and indicates the holy days of a particular religion. On such holy days, special rituals are performed to commemorate important events in a particular religion's history.

THE CELEBRATION OF FAITH

Catholicism – the Liturgical Year

The liturgical year is the annual journey through religious rituals in which Catholics:

- recall the events in the life of Jesus Christ and the beginnings of the Christian religion
- celebrate Jesus living in his church today
- are invited to grow closer to him in worship.

Advent
Advent starts the liturgical year. It is a four-week period leading up to Christmas, during which Christians reflect on their lives and prepare to celebrate Jesus's birth.

Christmas
This celebrates the birth of Jesus. The name comes from an Old English expression meaning the *mass of Christ*. The date of the feast itself is 25 December, but the exact time of year when Jesus was born is unknown. It includes the feast of the *Epiphany* (which commemorates the Magi worshipping the infant Jesus).

Ordinary time
This covers sixty per cent of the liturgical year and is divided into two periods. It focuses on different aspects of Jesus's life and teachings, especially the parables and miracles.

Lent

This is a period lasting forty days (not including Sundays), beginning on Ash Wednesday, which is a time of preparation for Easter. It should involve prayer, fasting and doing charitable works.

Easter

This is the most important part of the liturgical year. All the other events in Jesus's life derive their significance from his having died and risen from the dead. It is a moveable feast that must be celebrated on the first Sunday after the first full moon after the Spring Equinox (between 22 March and 25 April). It includes the feasts of the Ascension and Pentecost (the birthday of Christian religion).

Judaism – Religious Festivals

TABLE 7.5

Rosh Hashanah	Marks start of Jewish New Year.
Yom Kippur	Period of fasting lasting 24 hours. Time for reflection and for seeking God's forgiveness.
Sukkot (Tabernacles)	Commemorates how God cared for Jews as they travelled through the desert to the Promised Land.
Hannukah (Festival of Lights)	Held in winter to commemorate the re-dedication of the Temple in 165 B.C. and to celebrate the survival of Judaism in spite of great persecution.
Shavuoth (Feast of Weeks)	Celebrates God giving the Ten Commandments to Moses.
Pesach (Passover)	Seven-day festival in Israel, but lasts eight days elsewhere. Commemorates God freeing the Jews from captivity in Egypt. High point of this festival is the *Seder* (Passover Meal).

THE CELEBRATION OF FAITH

Islam — Religious Festivals

Key points are as follows.

- Although the Islamic calendar has twelve months, it follows the *lunar cycle* (the time between one full moon and the next). As a result, the Muslim year is eleven days shorter than that of Jews and Christians.
- Muslims date their era from A.D. 622, the year Muhammad emigrated from Makkah to Madinah.
- *Eid* or *id* is the Arabic word for *festival*.
- An Islamic festival is a large-scale communal celebration designed to encourage friendship and goodwill. Gifts are exchanged and traditionally food is donated to the poor.

TABLE 7.6: Important Islamic Festivals

Hijrah	Marks beginning of Muslim year. Recalls Muhammad's leaving Makkah for Madinah.
Ramadan	Commemorates Muhammad receiving the Qur'an from Allah. People fast during daylight hours.
Eid-ul-Fitr	Celebrates end of Ramadan.
Eid-ul-Adha	Held in final month of Muslim year. Celebrates completion of Hajj and commemorates Abraham's complete submission to the will of Allah — an example for all Muslims to follow.

Buddhism – Religious Festivals

Buddhists follow a lunar calendar, but each branch of Buddhism has its own version. Generally speaking, all date the origin of their religion to 544 B.C., when the Buddha is believed to have died.

The Buddha himself seems to have taught that festivals were of little importance. However, over the centuries Buddhists developed a number of festivals to commemorate and celebrate important aspects of his life and teaching.

Two important Buddhist festivals are *Wesak* and *Kathina*.

Wesak celebrates the birth, enlightenment and death of the Buddha. It is held in May, or in June during a leap year. Lay people visit temples and light candles to symbolise Buddha's enlightenment. Gifts are exchanged and parties are organised for children.

Kathina is the festival of giving that occurs at the end of Asalha (the rainy season). It comes after a period of three months' quiet meditation for monks and nuns. At the end of this, the members of a sangha ask each other for forgiveness for any ways in which they have offended each other. Lay people go to the sanghas and offer practical gifts (e.g. cloth and food) to the monks and nuns.

PILGRIMAGE

Meaning

A *pilgrimage* is *a journey made by a believer to a place that his/her religion considers holy.*

A *pilgrim* is *a person who goes on a pilgrimage, either alone or as a member of a group.*

Places of Pilgrimage

A place may become a centre of pilgrimage for different reasons:

- it may be associated with some event in the life of a holy person or the founder of a particular religion
- it may be the burial place of such a person.

Usually pilgrims go to pray at a *shrine* – *a religious monument that commemorates an important event or holy person associated with that place.*
For example:

- the Kaaba in Makkah for Muslims
- the Via Dolorosa in Jerusalem for Christians.

People go on pilgrimage for a variety of reasons:

- to seek God's forgiveness for past sins
- to ask for God's guidance
- to gain strength from God
- to revitalise their faith.

THE CELEBRATION OF FAITH

Christian Places of Pilgrimage

The Holy Land is the most frequently visited pilgrimage site for Christians who want to retrace the footsteps of Jesus. The main sites are:

- Bethlehem – Church of the Nativity
- Nazareth – Basilica of the Annunciation
- Jerusalem – Via Dolorosa (Way of Sorrows) and Church of the Holy Sepulchre.

Another important centre is Rome, where the headquarters of the Catholic church is located in the Vatican. Important sites here include:

- Basilica of St Peter
- Sistine Chapel
- Catacombs.

Important pilgrimage sites in Ireland include:

- Croagh Patrick
- Lough Derg
- Downpatrick
- Knock.

Croagh Patrick

Located in Co. Mayo, Croagh Patrick has been a popular pilgrimage site since the Middle Ages. It is said to have been a place where St Patrick came to pray. Pilgrims are expected to walk barefoot along a steep four-kilometre track to the mountain top (some 765m above the surrounding countryside).

Knock

Knock is also located in Co. Mayo. It is a *Marian shrine*, a holy place dedicated to Mary, the mother of Jesus. It is said to have been the site of an apparition (appearance) of Mary on the evening of 21 August 1879. No message was given but some people claimed to have been cured after visiting the site. Pope John Paul II celebrated mass there in 1979.

Buddhist Places of Pilgrimage

Buddhists believe that going on pilgrimage creates positive karma and so helps them to achieve a better life following their next reincarnation.

There are many Buddhist places of pilgrimage across Asia, but two of the most important are:

- *Bodh Gaya* in Bihar, where the Buddha achieved enlightenment
- *Sarnath* in Uttar Pradesh, where he gave his first sermon.

Many Buddhists try to visit a place associated with the Buddha, such as the Tooth Relic Temple in Kandy, Sri Lanka. This is said to have housed the Buddha's teeth since they were brought there in the fourth century B.C.

The Islamic Hajj

TABLE 7.7

Meaning	The *Hajj* is the pilgrimage to Makkah, Islam's holiest place.
Importance	It is the duty of every Muslim to make this journey at least once in his/her lifetime. An estimated 1.5 million do so each year.
Belief	Anyone who participates in the Hajj in a spirit of reverence will have his/her sins forgiven. Anyone who dies while journeying either to or from Makkah is declared a martyr and is immediately welcomed into paradise by Allah.
Preparations	On arrival in Makkah all pilgrims bathe and men put on the *ihram* to symbolise the equality of all men before Allah.
Route	1 Walk around Kaaba seven times anti-clockwise. Kiss/touch the black stone in centre. 2 Pass between the hills of Safa and Marwa seven times. Then drink from the Zamzam (well), which Allah made for Hagar and Ishmael. 3 Go to the Plain of Arafat and pray from noon to dusk. 4 Go to Mina and throw stones at the three pillars to symbolise rejection of the Devil. 5 Return to Makkah and walk seven times around the Kaaba.

The end of the Hajj is the feast of *Eid-ul-Adha* (a four-day festival).

The title *Hajji* is given to anyone who has completed the Hajj.

WORSHIP AS A RESPONSE TO MYSTERY

(Higher Level Only)

The Meaning of Mystery

A *mystery* is *a question to which human beings cannot find a complete answer, because the matter it raises is so deep and so profound that it surpasses our capacity to comprehend it fully.*

Examples:

- why do bad things happen to good people?
- how can a person find true and lasting happiness?
- what happens after death?

The major world religions teach that they can help people to grow in understanding and gain important insights into such profound mysteries. However, they warn that people will never know the full answer to any of these questions. Only God can fully understand and know the answers to these questions.

Revelation

According to such monotheistic religions as Judaism, Christianity and Islam, *revelation* is *the way in which God reaches out to human beings and reveals things about his nature that human beings could otherwise never know.*

Revelation is necessary because God is so totally different from anything else in human experience. (For example, human beings live in time while God does not; God is eternal.) As a result, if we were left to our own devices, human beings would know very little about God.

God has revealed his presence to human beings through:

- prayer and meditation
- sacred texts
- miracles.

Encounter with the Mystery of God

Example: God calls Moses (Judaism)
Exodus Chapter 3 states that God called Moses to begin his mission to free the Jewish people from captivity in Egypt and to lead them to the Promised Land.

God appeared to Moses in a strange and mysterious way as 'a blazing bush' which 'was not burnt up'.

In this account, God (Yahweh) is revealed to be both awe-inspiring and loving.

Worship as a Response to Mystery

Example: the Doctrine of Transubstantiation (Catholicism)
Context: the consecration during the Liturgy of the Eucharist at mass.

The Catholic church teaches that through the power of the Holy Spirit and the action of the bishop/priest, at the consecration:

- the bread ceases to be bread and becomes the body of Jesus
- the wine ceases to be wine and becomes the blood of Jesus.

This is called the doctrine of *transubstantiation.*

When Catholics receive the eucharist at Holy Communion in the form of the host (i.e. bread wafer), they are receiving the gift of the risen Jesus himself, who is as really present to them as he was to the disciples two thousand years ago.

Section F

8 The Moral Challenge

INTRODUCTION TO MORALITY

Meaning

Human beings are by nature social creatures whose lives consist of a complex web of relationships. These relationships can be considered under three headings:

- interpersonal – family and friends
- communal – school and parish
- global – God and environment.

If these relationships are to succeed and thrive, people need to consider the implications of their actions. This is why morality is important.

Morality may be defined as *a set of beliefs that offer people guidance about the rightness or wrongness of their actions.*

Human Actions

A distinction must be made between moral actions and non-moral actions. Morality is concerned only with moral actions, not with non-moral ones.

Non-moral Actions
Example: accidentally slipping and falling off a ladder.

Here the person does not make a free and deliberate choice. He/she is not in control of the action. Therefore the action is *non-moral*, i.e. neither morally right nor morally wrong.

Moral Actions
Example: rescuing someone from a burning building.

In this example the person does make a free and deliberate choice;

he/she is in control of their action. Therefore the action is *moral*: in this case morally right, since it results in saving another person's life.

People can be held responsible for the consequences of their *moral* actions, i.e. praised/rewarded if they are right/good and blamed/punished if they are wrong/bad.

The Role of Values

A person's moral actions are profoundly influenced by the *values* that he/she holds. Their values may lead them to perform certain actions or to avoid doing them altogether.

A *value* is *anything or anyone considered to be good, desirable, important or worthwhile.*

For example:

- a doctor who values her patients' lives and health will do her utmost to care for them
- a businessman who values dedicated and skilled workers will offer them the pay and conditions needed to retain them in his company.

Socialisation refers to *the process by which people acquire their values and learn how to behave towards others.*

At first, people usually derive their values from their family, but as they grow older they encounter a wider variety of influences on their values.

Influences on People's Values

Family
This is the first place where people learn how to interact with others. They normally learn to treat others with compassion and respect.

Friends
Genuine friendships can build up people's self-confidence and self-worth. They can help people to be more considerate towards others and give them the encouragement needed to do right rather than wrong.

School
Going to school provides people with an opportunity to develop their minds

THE MORAL CHALLENGE

and acquire the knowledge and skills needed to make the right choices when faced with difficult decisions.

Religion
This offers answers to life's great questions and can shape a person's whole outlook on life. It provides a code to help guide people's behaviour with a view towards making the world a better place for all.

The media
The media can powerfully affect people's priorities. They can encourage a self-centred approach to life, but if used wisely they can help people to be better informed about important issues and encourage them to be active participants rather than passive spectators.

The state
The state sets limits on people's behaviour by permitting certain activities and prohibiting others. However, people need to distinguish between what is legal and what is morally right. They are not always the same.

THE SOURCES OF MORALITY

Moral Vision

A moral vision is *the particular outlook on life that a person holds, based on his/her values, that motivates him/her to think and act in certain ways.*

A moral vision may be either *religious* (e.g. Christian or Muslim) or *non-religious* (e.g. humanist).

The Golden Rule

Whether their moral vision is religious or non-religious, all people of good character accept the Golden Rule as the fundamental principle of any system of morality.

In Judaism the Golden Rule is stated as 'Do unto others as you would have them do unto you.'

The basic idea of the Golden Rule is that people should have respect for and show compassion towards one another.

All religions have some version of this rule. However, there are sharp differences between them as to how it should be applied to particular moral issues such as abortion, capital punishment and war.

The Role of Religion

Traditionally, religion has been considered an important source of values and a trustworthy guide in matters of human conduct. All the major religions provide their members with a *code*, which may be defined as *a set of moral principles (fundamental truths) that the members of a religion should strive to put into practice in their daily lives.*

The Ten Commandments

This is one example of a religious code. The Ten Commandments are as follows:

> 1 I, the Lord, am your God; you shall have no other gods besides me.
> 2 You shall not take the name of the Lord your God in vain.
> 3 Remember to keep holy the Sabbath day.
> 4 Honour your father and your mother.
> 5 You shall not commit murder.
> 6 You shall not commit adultery.
> 7 You shall not steal.
> 8 You shall not bear false witness against your neighbour.
> 9 You shall not covet your neighbour's wife.
> 10 You shall not covet anything that belongs to your neighbour.
> Source: *The Catholic Faith Handbook*, St Mary's Press

These can be divided into two groups:

- the first three commandments set out what is meant by genuine love of God
- commandments four to ten deal with how people should love and respect one another.

The Ten Commandments provide the foundation for the moral teaching of the three great monotheistic religions – Judaism, Christianity and Islam.

THE MORAL CHALLENGE

Religious Authorities and Moral Guidance

Many of the world's religions state that their leaders have been given a special authority and a duty to guide their members as to how they should respond to moral issues.

Example: the Magisterium in the Catholic Church.

This is the official teaching authority of the Catholic Church. It consists of the Pope and the college of bishops under his leadership.

Catholics distinguish between the *Extraordinary* Magisterium and the *Ordinary* Magisterium.

Extraordinary Magisterium

Catholics believe that when the Pope speaks *ex cathedra* (using his full authority as successor to the apostle Peter) on matters of faith and morals, he is protected from error by the Holy Spirit. In this situation his statements are believed to be *infallible* (free from error) and must be accepted by all Catholics.

Ordinary Magisterium

This concerns *non-infallible* statements issued by the Pope offering guidance to Catholics on moral issues. Since Catholics believe that God continues to speak to them through the teachings of their church, they are expected to treat these statements with respect, carefully study and accept them.

A *papal encyclical* is the name given to a special letter written by the Pope that offers Catholics guidance about religious and moral issues.

GROWING IN MORALITY

How Moral Growth Occurs

We may define *moral growth* as *the process by which people acquire the knowledge of what is right and wrong and the ability to distinguish between them.*

Moral growth is a gradual process. From an early age people experience many influences on their moral development, including:

- family
- friends
- school

- religion
- the media
- clubs
- state services.

People learn what is right from what is wrong by:

- following the example set by people they trust, e.g. family and friends
- learning from the consequences of their own actions and those of others
- accepting the rules laid down by their parents, school, religion and society.

The Stages of Moral Growth

Stage 1: Infant
An infant is entirely self-centred. He/she is only aware of and seeks satisfaction for his/her immediate needs or wants, e.g. food, warmth and companionship.

Stage 2: Child
The child gradually begins to develop some understanding of right and wrong. He/she gains a greater awareness of how his/her actions have consequences for both his/herself and others. However, the expectation of reward or punishment largely determines his/her moral choices.

Stage 3: Young Adult/Teenager
A young adult should grow in self-confidence and self-worth. He/she should be able to distinguish right from wrong in more complex moral situations. However, peer group approval is a significant influence on his/her moral choices.

Moral Maturity

As a person grows older, he/she should become less preoccupied with material values (e.g. money and property) and develop a greater appreciation for spiritual values (e.g. love and compassion).

However, while age is important in the area of moral development, people do not automatically become more morally mature as they grow older.

THE MORAL CHALLENGE

A person can only achieve moral maturity when he/she is no longer motivated by:

- a selfish desire to satisfy his/her needs to the exclusion of those of others
- a fear of punishment or desire for reward
- a longing to gain the approval of others.

A morally mature person is one who has:

- a strong commitment to doing what is right
- a respect for both him/herself and others
- a willingness to stop, honestly evaluate the situation and consider the consequences before taking action
- the courage to actually do what he/she believes to be right.

Conscience

Conscience means a person's *ability to apply his/her values to a particular moral problem and make a decision about what the right thing to do is.*

We can identify three different kinds of conscience.

- *Properly informed.* This is when a person has achieved moral maturity. They seek to inform themselves as fully as possible before making any decision. The moral decision they make will be consistent with their values.
- *Lax.* This is when a person has consistently acted in selfish ways and has eventually desensitised him/herself to the whole issue of whether something is right or wrong.
- *Legalistic.* This is when a person's decision-making processes are dominated by a rigid, closed-minded, rule-keeping approach to life. While it can give some people a great sense of security, it can also make them blind to the right and appropriate course of action to follow.

Difficulties

To follow one's conscience in moral matters requires *courage* and *honesty*. Courage has been defined as *the ability to make a moral choice to do good, even if it is in opposition to other people who have power over you.*

Honesty involves:

- being truthful with oneself, God and others

- recognising one's obligation to do good even if it is not to one's own advantage
- rejecting lying, cheating and the desire to succeed at any price.

Even if a person is courageous and honest, he/she must be careful to ensure that he/she is not:

- being deliberately or unintentionally misled by someone
- making a decision based on false assumptions
- making an error in his/her reasoning.

MORALITY IN ACTION

Making a Moral Decision

When faced with an important moral decision, a person should ask him/herself the following questions:

- *Situation* – what exactly is the problem facing me?
- *Information* – do I have all the relevant facts?
- *Guidance* – where can I get reliable advice? What does the law say? What does my religion teach?
- *Motive* – what do I want to achieve?
- *Method* – what is the right way to achieve it?
- *Impact* – how will my actions affect other people?

One should make a moral decision and pursue a particular course of action only after going through this process.

Difficulties

Certain things can cloud a person's judgment and make it difficult to know what is the right choice. There are four main areas of difficulty.

1 When a person does not understand the true nature of the problem he/she faces.
2 When a person allows his/her emotions to have too great an influence on his/her decisions.
3 When a person only makes a particular choice in order to conform with or to win favour with others.
4 When a person makes a mistake in his/her moral reasoning.

THE MORAL CHALLENGE

The Influence of Moral Vision on the Decisions of Believers

Example 1: the Environment
The environment is *the world and everything in it*.
   The principal environmental problems facing humanity are:

- the destruction of the rainforests
- global warming
- nuclear waste
- acid rain.

The approach of Jews, Christians and Muslims to solving these problems is profoundly influenced by the moral vision they all share.
   The Tenakh, the Bible and the Qur'an all remind their readers that:

- the environment is a *gift* from God
- the environment is *sacred*, i.e. worthy of total respect
- human beings are not the owners of the environment but God's *stewards*
- humans have a special responsibility to care for the world on God's behalf and not give in to short-term and selfish interests.

Only by taking all this to heart can human beings develop a new relationship that will ensure that the earth is passed on in a healthy and fertile state to future generations.
   Practical steps that can be taken include:

- being less wasteful of resources
- recycling where possible
- using biodegradable products
- joining environmental protection groups
- voting for political candidates who are genuinely committed to protecting the environment.

Example 2: War
War may be defined as *armed hostilities between two groups in which each side puts people forward to fight and kill.*
   The consequences of war include:

- loss of human life
- physical and mental suffering of the survivors
- a refugee crisis

- destruction of property
- enormous debt.

Since all the great monotheistic religions teach that human life should be respected, they have devoted much effort to offering their members guidance about the awful reality of war.

One Christian response to the question of whether or not to engage in warfare is called the *Just War Theory*. This aims to:

- identify conditions under which it is morally right to go to war
- put limits as to how people should wage war so as to minimise the harm inflicted.

According to the Just War Theory, a Christian may only engage in warfare if six conditions can be fulfilled. These are:

1. *Just Cause*. The war must be one of defence against an unprovoked attack.
2. *Right Intention*. The aim of those going to war must be to restore peace and achieve reconciliation. It must not be an act of revenge.
3. *Last Resort*. All other options must have been explored without success, and all peaceful alternatives must have been exhausted.
4. *Likelihood of Success*. There must be a reasonable hope that the objectives for which the war is fought can be achieved.
5. *Principle of Proportion*. The war should not inflict more suffering than would be experienced by not going to war.
6. *Safety of Non-Combatants*. Civilians should never be the intended targets of the war. Nothing can justify the indiscriminate killing of civil populations.

It is important to remember that those Christians who believe it is sometimes necessary and unavoidable to go to war never accept it as a good thing. Human life can only flourish where there is peace.

LAW AND MORALITY

Law

A law is *a rule set out by the state authorities, permitting some forms of behaviour and prohibiting others, which its citizens are obliged to obey.*

A *legal* action is one that is *in accordance with* the law of the state.

THE MORAL CHALLENGE

An *illegal* action is one that *violates* the law of the state.

Rights
By *rights* we mean *the basic entitlements people need to promote and defend their dignity as human beings.*
Important rights include:

- the right to life
- the right to a fair trial
- the right to join a trade union.

A full list of human rights can be found in the *Universal Declaration on Human Rights*, approved by the United Nations Organisation in 1948.

Religious Morality and the Law

All the major world religions teach that their members should strive to be good citizens of whatever state they live in. However, they also caution them to remember that:

- the state does not have the final say as to what is right and what is wrong
- there is a higher standard for distinguishing right from wrong, which is set by God.

Therefore, a person should not blindly obey the laws of the state. Indeed, a state can sometimes wrongly use the law to deprive people of their rights, for example the apartheid regime in South Africa in the late twentieth century. A person should obey the law of the state only if it is the morally right thing to do. Sometimes it is necessary to disobey a particular law in order to highlight an injustice and replace it with a just law. For example, black people in America, led by Dr Martin Luther King, conducted a campaign of non-violent protest to resist unjust laws that deprived them of important civil rights (mid-twentieth century).

There are three different views as to how far religious morality should influence the law of the state.

1 *Fundamentalism.* The laws of a particular state should be based entirely on the moral code of its dominant religion and no other point of view should be tolerated.

2 *Pluralism.* No one group should be allowed to dominate and all different groups should have equal influence. The aim is for the state's laws to encourage the different groups (races, religions etc.) to live together in peace and preserve their own distinctive customs.
3 *Libertarianism.* People should be free to live as they choose with only minimum restrictions imposed on them by the state: in particular, in exercising their individual rights they should not interfere with the rights of others.

Law in Islam

The ideal Muslim society is a *theocracy*, i.e. a state governed by laws based on the teachings of Islam.

Over the centuries, Islamic leaders and scholars have compiled an all-embracing code of morality and law called the *Shari'a*. All Muslims are expected to faithfully observe the Shari'a. Most countries with an Islamic majority legally prohibit and make punishable the following:

- adultery
- consumption of alcohol
- astrology
- gambling
- use of unprescribed drugs
- prostitution
- dancing between men and women.

Muslims strongly defend the Shari'a against the charge that it is too harsh. They point out that:

- statistics for crime and violence are much lower in Islamic countries than in non-Islamic ones
- non-Muslims living in a Muslim state do not have to become Muslims. However, they must abide by Islamic law.

Glossary

agnosticism the belief that it is impossible for human beings to know if God exists or not.

ascetic a person who lives a life of prayer and self-denial.

atheism the belief that God does not exist.

blasphemy any action or statement that displays grave disrespect toward God.

Buddha the title given to Siddhartha Gautama, the founder of Buddhism. It means 'the Enlightened One'.

Christian a follower of Jesus Christ. From the Greek word for 'Messiah' – 'Christos'.

church a community of Christians or the place where they meet.

code a set of guidelines for living offered by a particular religion, which helps people to decide what is the right or the wrong thing to do, e.g. the Ten Commandments.

community this exists wherever people
- live or work together
- share similar interests
- hold broadly similar views about life.

community of faith a group of people with a religion in common.

conscience a person's ability to apply his/her values to a particular moral problem and make a decision about what the right thing to do is.

convert to change from one religion to another.

covenant the sacred agreement that God made with the Jewish people.

creed a set of beliefs shared by the members of a religion about God and the meaning of life.

denomination refers to one of the branches of the Christian religion.

doctrine the official teaching of a religion.

ecumenism the movement that attempts to foster a sense of togetherness across the centuries-old divisions that separate the different Christian denominations from one another.

evangelist means 'proclaimer of the good news'. It is the title given to an author of a gospel (Mark, Matthew, Luke and John).

evolution the scientific theory that states that all life – plant, animal and human – has developed by the process of natural selection from simpler to more complex forms over the course of millions of years.

faith involves:
- belief in God
- love of God
- belief in the truth of God's revelation
- trust in God's goodness.

formal prayer this can be either prayer with a fixed format that has been taken from the sacred text of a religion (e.g. the Our Father from the gospels), or decided upon by the leaders of a particular religion (e.g. the Apostle's Creed).

fundamentalist in relation to a sacred text, this refers to someone who will only accept a *literal* (word for word) reading of it.

gentile term used to describe a non-Jew.

heresy what the leaders of a religion consider to be false teachings about God.

human rights the basic entitlements that each person needs to promote and defend his/her dignity as a human being.

icon from the Greek word meaning 'image'. Icons are richly decorated paintings of Jesus, Mary or some other religious figure(s). They use symbolism to make visible the invisible world of God, the angels and saints.

idolatry the worship of anyone or anything other than God.

GLOSSARY

incarnation the belief that in Jesus of Nazareth, God became a human being. Jesus is both fully human and fully divine.

Islam an Arabic word meaning 'peace through submission to the revealed will of Allah'. The world's second-largest organised religion.

law a rule set out by the state authorities permitting some forms of behaviour and prohibiting others, which its citizens are obliged to obey.

legalism harsh and excessive devotion to the precise letter of the law.

martyr a person who has died for his/her beliefs.

materialism a way of life that seeks fulfilment through acquiring material wealth.

meditation an inner quietness that allows a person to focus his/her whole attention on the mystery of God's love and on how he/she should respond to it.

Messiah the saviour whom the Jews believed God would send to them.

miracle a marvellous or wonderful event that occurs solely as a result of God's direct action. The gospels identify four kinds:
- healing miracles
- nature miracles
- exorcisms
- restorations to life.

missionary a person who is sent to spread the teachings of a religion.

monotheism the belief that there is only one God.

morality a set of beliefs that offer people guidance about the rightness or wrongness of human actions.

moral action any action that is deliberate, freely chosen and under the control of the person doing it.

Muslim name given to member of the Islamic religion. It means 'one who submits'.

mystery a question to which human beings cannot find a complete answer, e.g. 'Why do bad things happen to good people?' The major religions help people to gain insights into and grow in their understanding of life's mysteries.

nirvana according to Hindus, this is a state of complete happiness and perfect peace.

oral tradition important stories and teachings passed on from one generation to the next by word of mouth.

parable an image or story in which a person illustrates some part of his/her message by using concrete examples drawn from everyday life.
Examples of Jesus's parables include:
- the Good Samaritan
- the Unforgiving Servant.

patriarch this can refer to either:
- a founding father of Judaism, e.g. Abraham or Moses; *or*
- a leader of an Orthodox Church, e.g. the Patriarch of Moscow (Russian Orthodox Church) or the Patriarch of Constantinople (Greek Orthodox Church).

pilgrimage a journey made by a believer to a place that his/her religion considers holy.

polytheism the belief in more than one god, e.g. Hinduism.

prayer a conversation from the heart between God and human beings. It is vital for building a strong and lasting relationship with God.

problem a question to which human beings can find a complete answer, e.g. 'How is electricity generated?'

prophet a holy man who has received messages from God, which he then preaches to people, e.g. Elijah in the Old Testament and John the Baptist in the New Testament.

pulpit a raised platform used for speaking/giving a sermon.

religion belief in and worship of a God or gods.

reincarnation the belief that human beings must endure a long cycle of birth, death and rebirth before they can achieve nirvana.

GLOSSARY

repent to show sorrow for one's sins and to change one's way of life for the better.

resurrection the Christian teaching that Jesus rose from the dead on Easter Sunday after dying on the cross on Good Friday.

revelation the way in which God communicates with human beings and tells them things about who God is and how they should live, which they would otherwise not know.

reverence deep respect for someone or something.

ritual a religious ceremony that:
- gives a regular pattern to people's worship of God
- celebrates the mysterious and invisible presence of God in people's lives through the use of symbols.

sacrament a public ritual in which Christians recall and re-enact the life, death and resurrection of Jesus Christ. According to the Catholic and Orthodox traditions there are seven sacraments:
- baptism
- confirmation
- eucharist
- reconciliation
- matrimony
- holy orders
- anointing the sick.

sacred something deserving of people's total respect, e.g. human life; the world people share.

sacred text the holy book or scriptures of a particular religion, e.g. the Bible (Christianity), the Qur'an (Islam).

sacrifice offering something of value to God in worship.

science any area of study in which knowledge is gained by observation, experiment and reasoning.

secularism the decline in active membership of organised religion and the lessening of religion's influence on many people's values.

Shahadah the creed that all Muslims are expected to recite: 'There is no God but Allah and Muhammad is his prophet.'

Shari'a an all-embracing code of morality and law that all Muslims are expected to observe faithfully.

sign any concrete image, word or gesture that points beyond itself but has only one meaning, e.g. a traffic light at a road junction.

sin any freely chosen, deliberate act that damages or destroys one's relationship with God and other people.

socialisation the way in which people learn to behave towards others.

symbol any concrete image, word or gesture that points beyond itself and has more than one meaning, e.g. the lights on a Christmas tree or a nation's flag.

theism the belief that God exists.

theocracy a state governed by laws based on the teachings of one particular religion.

transubstantiation the Catholic belief that at the consecration during the mass, while the outward appearances remain the same, the bread ceases to be bread and becomes the body of Jesus, and the wine ceases to be wine and becomes the blood of Jesus.

Trinity the belief that there are three persons in one God.

value anything or anyone considered to be good, desirable, important or worthwhile.

Vatican headquarters of the Catholic Church.

vocation The sense a person has of being called by God to do something worthwhile in life.

worship any action by which people show that they recognise the supreme importance of God as the creator and sustainer of the universe.

Exam Papers
Junior Certificate Examinations 2006 & 2007

Coimisiún na Scrúduithe Stáit
State Examinations Commission

JUNIOR CERTIFICATE EXAMINATION, 2006
RELIGIOUS EDUCATION — HIGHER LEVEL

Total Marks: 400
THURSDAY, 15 JUNE – AFTERNOON, 2.00 to 4.00

SECTION 1 (50 marks)
YOU SHOULD SPEND ABOUT 15 MINUTES ANSWERING QUESTIONS IN THIS SECTION.
YOU MUST ATTEMPT **TEN** OF THE FOLLOWING TWENTY QUESTIONS.
IN QUESTIONS WHERE YOU ARE REQUIRED TO TICK ✓ THE CORRECT BOX, TICK **ONE** BOX ONLY.
(All questions carry 5 marks each)

1. One parable from the gospels that Jesus told is (Tick ✓ the correct box)

   Daniel in the Lion's Den ☐ The Burning Bush ☐

   The Good Samaritan ✓ The Raising of Jairus' Daughter ☐

2. Moderator is the title of a leader associated with the Presbyterian Church
   (Tick ✓ the correct box)

   True ✓   False ☐

3. Read the list of religious symbols and the list of world religions given below. One religious symbol has been matched to the religion which it is associated as an example for you. Make **one** other match.

Religious Symbols	Religions
Aum	Buddhism
Cross	Christianity
Menorah	Hinduism
Mihrab	Islam
Prayer Wheel	Judaism

Example:

Cross	Christianity

Answer:

Menorah	Judaism

4. In religious traditions sectarianism means – *To have hatred for an individual or group based on religion.*

5. According to the Gospels, **one** person Jesus appeared to after his death and resurrection was *Thomas*.

6. A libertarian holds the view that everyone should be free to do as he/she chooses, so long as he/she does not interfere with the equal freedom of others. (Tick ✓ the correct box)

   True ✓   False ☐

7. A key person in the founding story of Judaism is – (Tick ✓ the correct box)

   Abraham ✓   Gandhi ☐   Gautama ☐   Jesus ☐

8. In religious traditions ministry means

9. Clonmacnoise is a place of religious importance in Ireland. Name another place of religious importance in Ireland *Knock*

10. In religious traditions a division or major split between people of the same faith is known as a *Schism*

11. Zakat is an important part of the moral code of Islam.
    (Tick ✓ the correct box)

    True ☐   False ☐

12. Read the list of religious celebrations and the list of world religions given below. One celebration has been matched to the religion with which it is associated as an example for you. Make **one** other match.

Religious Celebrations	Religions
Diwali	Buddhism
Easter	Christianity
Eid-al-fitr	Hinduism
Rosh Hashanah	Islam
Wesak	Judaism

    Example:

Easter	Christianity

    Answer:

Rosh Hashanah	Judaism

13. Atheism means to believe there is no God.

14. A prayer of penitence is a prayer which expresses sorrow for sin.
    (Tick ✓ the correct box)

    True ✓   False ☐

15. Pluralism holds the view that

16. At the time of Jesus, Jerusalem was in the province of

17. Which **one** of the following world religions is an example of polytheism? (Tick ✓ the correct box)

    Christianity ☐   Hinduism ✓   Islam ☐   Judaism ☐

18. To behave morally means — To behave knowing the difference between right & wrong.

19. A sacrament is

20. One factor which influences religious practice is

SECTION 2 (30 marks)
YOU SHOULD SPEND ABOUT 15 MINUTES ANSWERING QUESTIONS IN THIS SECTION.
CHOOSE **THREE** OF THE FOLLOWING PHOTOGRAPHS AND ANSWER THE QUESTIONS ON EACH.
(All questions carry 10 marks each)

Question 1. This is a photograph of an ecumenical gathering.

Focolare Movement

A. Pick **one** thing from the photograph which shows that this is an ecumenical gathering.
(2 marks)

B. What is ecumenism?
(4 marks)

C. Give **two** other examples of ecumenism in action.
(4 marks)

Question 2. This drawing is based on the miracle of Jesus raising Lazarus from the dead.

Adapted from Octopus Books Limited

A. Pick **one** thing from the drawing which shows how people reacted to the miracles of Jesus.

(2 marks)

B. Name **one** other miracle that Jesus performed.

(4 marks)

C. State **two** characteristics of the kingdom of God that can be seen in one of Jesus' miracles.

(4 marks)

Question 3. This drawing shows a moral code.

1. I am the Lord your God: You shall have no other gods before me.
2. You shall not make wrongful use of the name of the Lord your God.
3. Remember the Sabbath day and keep it holy.
4. Honour your father and your mother.
5. You shall not murder.
6. You shall not commit adultery.
7. You shall not steal.
8. You shall not bear false witness against your neighbour.
9. You shall not covet your neighbour's house.
10. You shall not covet your neighbour's wife.

Ex. 20:3, 7, 8, 12, 13-17.

Adapted from Softkey Multimedia Inc.

A. Explain why this is an example of a moral code.

(4 marks)

B. Name **one** religious moral code.

(2 marks)

C. Give **two** reasons why a moral code is important in a community of faith.

(4 marks)

Question 4. This is a photograph of a young person taking part in a Sacred Thread ceremony.

www.swaminarayan.org

A. Pick **one** thing from the photograph which shows that this ceremony is celebrating religious faith.

(3 marks)

B. Name **one** other ceremony which celebrates a stage in the growth of religious faith.

(3 marks)

C. Taking part in a religious ceremony is one way of expressing religious faith. Name **two** other ways of expressing religious faith.

(4 marks)

SECTION 3 (50 marks)
YOU SHOULD SPEND ABOUT 15 MINUTES ANSWERING QUESTIONS IN THIS SECTION.
READ THE FOLLOWING EXTRACT FROM A LETTER AND ANSWER ALL THE QUESTIONS BELOW.

".... I'm just back from the Christmas Carol Service. Even though it was cold, just about everyone was there. When we all stood to sing 'O Come All Ye Faithful' I thought of you; I know it's your favourite Christmas carol.

The children from the local school decorated a Christmas tree with special symbols. Each symbol stood for a person from the Bible who was looking forward to the coming of the Messiah. All the parents looked very proud watching their children place stars, harps, etc. on the branches of the tree. Two teenagers read a commentary about each of the people represented on this special tree, which is called a Jesse tree.

Rev. Farrell read modern poems and prayers, as well as readings from the

Bible. The whole community was represented in the procession to put the figures into the crib. The figures of Mary and Joseph were carried by a newly married couple who have just moved here. I thought it was nice to include them in that way. Members of a local band even wrote their own carol for the occasion.

You could see that it meant a lot to everyone.

We lit candles for friends and family members who weren't with us. I lit a candle for you, all those miles away. I didn't need to say anything. Just lighting the candle, and watching its flame, was enough for me to know that you would have a good Christmas too.

When I shook hands with people as a sign of peace, lots of people asked me to give you their best wishes and to wish you a happy Christmas. During the sign of peace the local youth group brought up boxes of toys and food which they had collected for people in need.

I hope you liked the present I sent you. I also included a tiny bit of straw from the crib. I'm sure you were wondering what it was. I thought it would remind you of all those you know, who love you and who are thinking about you as they celebrate Christmas…"

1. What evidence is there in this letter to suggest that Christmas is a time of religious importance?

    (12 marks)

2. a. What evidence is there in this letter to show that the carol service was an example of communal prayer?

    (10 marks)

    b. Give **one** example of a symbol that was used during the carol service and explain what it means.

    (10 marks)

3. Give **two** reasons why people worship.

    (6 marks)

4. How does this letter show what is meant by **one** of the following:

    • Religious belief   • Wonder

    (12 marks)

SECTION 4 (200 marks)
YOU SHOULD SPEND ABOUT 55 MINUTES ANSWERING QUESTIONS IN THIS SECTION.
YOU MUST ATTEMPT **FOUR** OF THE FOLLOWING SIX QUESTIONS.
(All questions carry 50 marks each)

Question 1. COMMUNITIES OF FAITH

A. Name a church **or** a religious organisation **or** a religious order found in present day Ireland, and outline **two** ways in which its beliefs influence the way of life of its members.

Name of church / religious organisation / religious order

(24 marks)

B. a. Outline **one** challenge that a church **or** a religious organisation **or** a religious order faces in Ireland today.

(10 marks)

b. Briefly outline how the beliefs of the church **or** the religious organisation **or** the religious order you have named above could help its members to deal with this challenge.

(16 marks)

Question 2. PALESTINE AT THE TIME OF JESUS

A. a. In the spaces marked on the map of Palestine below write –
- The name of the city shown at a)
- The names of the seas shown at b) and c).

(6 marks)

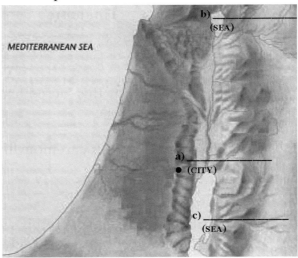

b. Name an important event in the life of Jesus which happened in **one** of the places you have named above.

Name of place   Name of event

(10 marks)

c. Briefly outline what happened in the event you have named.

(10 marks)

B. a. Outline what the Jewish people expected the Messiah to be like at the time of Jesus.

(10 marks)

b. Outline **one** way in which Jesus was like the Messiah that the Jewish people were expecting at the time.

(7 marks)

c. Outline **one** way in which Jesus was not like the Messiah that the Jewish people were expecting at the time.

(7 marks)

Question 3. STORIES OF FAITH

A. a. Tick ✓ **one** of the following world religions you have studied and name the sacred text associated with it:

Buddhism ☐   Hinduism ☐   Islam ☐   Judaism ☐

Name of sacred text

(5 marks)

b. Briefly explain why this sacred text is a document of faith.

(10 marks)

B. a. Outline **one** religious ceremony in which the sacred text you have named above is used.

(10 marks)

b. Describe **two** ways in which this sacred text influences the way of life of a follower of this world religion.

(10 marks)

C. • Buddhism • Hinduism • Islam • Judaism
Briefly describe a time of growth and development in **one** of the above world religions.

(15 marks)

Question 4. THE SEARCH FOR MEANING

A. Briefly explain how religious faith can grow out of the questions that a person asks in his/her search for meaning.

(16 marks)

B. Describe **two** other factors that can influence personal faith.

(16 marks)

C. People today express the search for meaning in many ways. Give **two** examples of how the search for meaning is expressed in today's world and give a brief account of each example.

(18 marks)

Question 5. PRAYER
A.

"When I worry I pray... I feel guilty praying because I'm always asking for something..."

"Silence plays a big role for me in prayer, because if you listen hard enough you will hear God speak back to you."

Source: Veritas

Why is prayer important in the life of a person who has religious belief?

(15 marks)

B.   Buddhism ☐   Christianity ☐   Hinduism ☐
Islam ☐   Judaism ☐

Tick ✓ **one** world religion you have studied from those listed above and name the place of worship where members of this world religion regularly gather for prayer.

   a.   Name of place of worship (5 marks)

   b.   Describe the place of worship you have named above.

   (15 marks)

   c.   Explain how the place of worship you have described above can help people to pray.

   (15 marks)

Question 6. MORALITY

A.   What is moral maturity?

   (14 marks)

B.   Family, friends, religion, etc. can influence a person's idea of what is right and wrong.
Outline how any **two** such influences can affect a person's idea of right and wrong.

   (16 marks)

C.   In making a decision, how would a morally mature person deal with the many influences on his/her idea of right and wrong.

   (20 marks)

SECTION 5 (70 marks)
YOU SHOULD SPEND ABOUT 20 MINUTES ANSWERING
QUESTIONS IN THIS SECTION.
YOU MUST ATTEMPT **ONE** OF THE FOLLOWING SIX QUESTIONS.
(All questions carry 70 marks each)

Question 1.
a. Outline **one** example of inter-faith dialogue that you have studied.
b. Discuss the reasons why people take part in inter-faith dialogue.

Question 2.
- Son of God
- Son of Man

Outline what **one** of the above titles shows about the early Christians' understanding of Jesus.

Question 3.
- Buddhism
- Hinduism
- Islam
- Judaism

Discuss how the style of leadership in **one** of the above world religions is influenced by the views of its founder/earliest followers.

Question 4.
Religion and science have points in common and points of difference in their understanding of creation.

Outline **one** point in common and **one** point of difference.

Question 5.
Communal prayer and worship show what a community believes and values.

Discuss this statement referring to **one** community of faith you have studied.

Question 6.
Discuss how *either* the search for truth *or* the search for peace has been a driving force in the life of a person of faith in a world religion you have studied

Coimisiún na Scrúduithe Stáit
State Examinations Commission

JUNIOR CERTIFICATE EXAMINATION, 2007
RELIGIOUS EDUCATION — HIGHER LEVEL

Total Marks: 400
THURSDAY, 14 JUNE – AFTERNOON, 2.00 to 4.00

SECTION 1 (50 marks)
YOU SHOULD SPEND ABOUT 15 MINUTES ANSWERING QUESTIONS IN THIS SECTION.
YOU MUST ATTEMPT **TEN** OF THE FOLLOWING TWENTY QUESTIONS.
IN QUESTIONS WHERE YOU ARE REQUIRED TO TICK ✓ THE CORRECT BOX,
TICK **ONE** BOX ONLY.
(All questions carry 5 marks each)

1. In religious traditions 'reconciliation' means

2. Galilee was a province in Palestine at the time of Jesus.
   (Tick ✓ the correct box)
   True ✓   False ☐

3. Polytheism is the belief in *Multiple gods*.

4. The title 'Rabbi' is most associated with a leader in which of the following world religions? (Tick ✓ the correct box)
   Buddhism ☐   Hinduism ☐   Judaism ✓

5. In religious traditions a 'vocation' is a calling to *prayer*

6. A Mosque is a place of worship associated with Hinduism.
   (Tick ✓ the correct box)
   True ☐   False ✓

7. Agnosticism holds the view that

8. Read the list of places of pilgrimage and the list of world religions given below. One place of pilgrimage has been matched to the religion with which it is most associated as an example for you. Make **one** other match.

Places of Pilgrimage	World Religions
Bethlehem	Buddhism
Bodh Gaya	Christianity
Mecca	Hinduism
River Ganges	Islam
Wailing Wall/Western Wall	Judaism

   Example: | Bethlehem | Christianity |
   Answer: | wailing wall | Judaism |

9. For a religious person 'sin' involves

10. The Five Pillars are associated with which **one** of the following world religions?   (Tick ✓ the correct box)

    Buddhism ✓   Islam ☐   Judaism ☐

11. In religious traditions to have 'authority' means

12. Croagh Patrick is a place of religious importance in Ireland. Name another place of religious importance in Ireland Knock

13. The Law of Karma is associated with Islam.   (Tick ✓ the correct box)

    True ☐   False ✓

14. In religious traditions 'petition' is a type of prayer that involves

15. An example of a meal Jesus shared with another person is
    (Tick ✓ the correct box)

    The Calming of the Storm ☐   The Good Samaritan ☐
    The Meeting with Zacchaeus ✓

16. In religious traditions a 'denomination' is

17. Humanism holds the view that

18. The Gospel of Mark is a synoptic gospel.   (Tick ✓ the correct box)

   True ☐   False ☐

19. Communication is a characteristic of communities.
    Name another characteristic of communities

20. A person uses his/her conscience to *form an opinion.*

SECTION 2 (30 marks)
YOU SHOULD SPEND ABOUT 15 MINUTES ANSWERING QUESTIONS IN THIS SECTION.
CHOOSE **THREE** OF THE FOLLOWING PHOTOGRAPHS AND ANSWER THE QUESTIONS ON EACH.
(All questions carry 10 marks each)

Question 1. This is a photograph of a religious sister serving the needs of others.

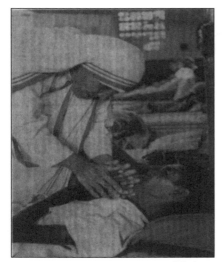

Veritas

A. Pick **one** thing from the photograph which suggests that this religious sister is serving the needs of others.
(2 marks)

B. Name **one** example of a community.
(2 marks)

C. Suggest **two** reasons why people need to live in a community.
(6 marks)

Question 2. This drawing is based on the Last Supper.

Octopus Books Ltd.

A. Pick **one** thing from the drawing which shows that this is the Last Supper.

(2 marks)

B. On which of the following days of the week did Jesus celebrate the Last Supper? (Tick ✓ the correct box)

Wednesday ☐   Thursday ☐   Friday ☐

(2 marks)

C. Give **two** reasons why the Last Supper was important for the first Christians.

(6 marks)

Question 3. This photograph shows an example of stewardship.

www.conservancy.bc.ca

A. Pick **one** thing from the photograph which shows that this is an example of stewardship.

(2 marks)

B. What is stewardship?

(4 marks)

C. Give **two** other examples of stewardship.

(4 marks)

Question 4. This is a photograph of people practising their religion.

Flame Tree Publishing

A. Pick **one** thing from this photograph which shows that these people are practising their religion.

(2 marks)

B. Give **one** reason why people practise their religion in this way.

(2 marks)

C. State **two** other ways in which people can practise their religion.

(6 marks)

SECTION 3 (50 marks)
YOU SHOULD SPEND ABOUT 15 MINUTES ANSWERING QUESTIONS IN THIS SECTION.
READ THE FOLLOWING EXTRACT FROM A LETTER AND ANSWER ALL THE QUESTIONS BELOW.

Hi God,
It's me. I know you don't normally hear from me but my teacher asked me to drop you a line.

It's all good though – I'm not my usual bored self! I'm just back from a retreat. I thought it would be boring, but everyone had to go so I went.

Well, it wasn't boring at all; it was great! We did all these group things that were really cool. Some of the talks we had were so funny. Even when people got serious about things in life everyone was listening. We talked with each other in small groups about life and what is important to us. I said stuff I never said out loud before. What I found cool about the day was that people listened to what I said. They really showed consideration for me and I also listened hard to what they said about their lives. We all found out a lot about each other. There was a real sense of caring among the group. It sounds funny for me to be talking this way, but I have to say it was really good.

We also had quiet times during the retreat when nobody spoke and we could just think about our feelings and what we valued in life. During the prayer service, we listened to a song, 'Rejoice in the Lord always'. Everyone was smiling a lot and the song really suited how we were feeling. Then we all had a chance to say things we liked about our lives. Lots of people remembered different things they were thankful for. Someone even mentioned that something I said was a help to them. I was really pleased that someone spoke so highly of what I had said.

The things people were happy about just piled up and up and everybody just wanted to hear more and more.

I really enjoyed the retreat. I definitely wasn't bored.
Thank you God for all that happened.
Sam

(Source: Adapted from Saint Mary's Press)

1.   Reflection ☐   Respect ☐

   Tick ✓ **one** of the above words and outline how this letter shows what it means.

   (15 marks)

2. Give **one** reason why it is important for members of a community of faith you have studied to show respect.

   (10 marks)

3.   Prayer of Praise ☐   Prayer of Thanksgiving ☐

   Tick ✓ **one** of the above types of prayer that you have studied.
   Outline what is involved in the type of prayer you have ticked above.

   (10 marks)

4.   • Prayer of Praise   • Prayer of Thanksgiving

   Outline how **one** of the above types of prayer can be seen in this letter.

   (15 marks)

SECTION 4 (200 marks)
YOU SHOULD SPEND ABOUT 55 MINUTES ANSWERING
QUESTIONS IN THIS SECTION.
YOU MUST ATTEMPT **FOUR** OF THE FOLLOWING SIX QUESTIONS.
(All questions carry 50 marks each)

Question 1. COMMUNITIES OF FAITH

A. Giving direction is one way a person can lead a community. Outline what is involved in **two** other ways of leading a community that could be used by a leader.

(20 marks)

B. Explain how the way in which a community is led can have an effect on its members.

(20 marks)

C. Being a leader is one role a person can have within a community. Describe **another** role a person can have within a community.

(10 marks)

Question 2. FOUNDATIONS OF RELIGION - CHRISTIANITY

A. Describe **one** incident from the life of Jesus that led to his death.

(15 marks)

B. Outline **two** reasons why the incident you have described above led to the death of Jesus.

(20 marks)

C. Outline how Jesus' death affected the people who were following him.

(15 marks)

Question 3. FOUNDATIONS OF RELIGION - MAJOR WORLD RELIGIONS

A.   Buddhism ☐   Hinduism ☐   Islam ☐   Judaism ☐
Tick ✓ **one** of the world religions above that you have studied.
   a. Name **one** key person/group of people associated with the founding story of the world religion you have ticked above

(5 marks)

b. Explain why the person/group of people you have named is important in the founding story of the world religion you have ticked above.

(10 marks)

B. Outline **one** way in which the story of the earliest followers influences members today in the world religion you have ticked above.

(15 marks)

C. Explain how the world religion you have ticked above is linked to another major world religion.

(20 marks)

Question 4. THE QUESTION OF FAITH

A. *People sometimes have experiences which make them wonder about the meaning of life.*
Describe how an experience in life could make a person ask questions about the meaning of life.

(20 marks)

B. a. Materialism ☐   Secularism ☐
Tick ✓ **one** of the above and describe what it means.

(10 marks)

b. Explain how the religious faith of a person could be challenged by *either* materialism *or* secularism.

(20 marks)

Question 5. THE CELEBRATION OF FAITH

A. a. Give **one** example of a symbol people use when they are praying

(5 marks)

b. Explain why people use the symbol you have given above when they are praying.

(9 marks)

B. Suggest **two** reasons why people can sometimes find it difficult to pray.

(12 marks)

C. a.   Meditation ☐   Penitence ☐

      Tick ✓ **one** of the above types of prayer that you have studied. Outline what is involved in the type of prayer you have ticked above.

(10 marks)

  b. Outline **two** reasons why prayer is important for members of a world religion that you have studied.

(14 marks)

Question 6. THE MORAL CHALLENGE

A. Outline what is involved in **two** stages of the process a person goes through in making a moral decision.

(18 marks)

B. a. Give **one** example of a situation where there could be conflict between a country's law and a religion.

(12 marks)

  b.   Pluralism ☐   Religious Fundamentalism ☐

     Tick ✓ **one** of the above and outline how it sees the relationship between a country's law and a religion.

(20 marks)

SECTION 5 (70 marks)
YOU SHOULD SPEND ABOUT 20 MINUTES ANSWERING QUESTIONS IN THIS SECTION.
YOU MUST ATTEMPT **ONE** OF THE FOLLOWING SIX QUESTIONS.
(All questions carry 70 marks each)

Question 1.
Outline how a community of faith you have studied shows a sense of -
i. Commitment.
ii. Vision.

Question 2.
Outline **two** historical sources of information about the life of Jesus of Nazareth and discuss the ways in which they are similar to what the gospels say about his life and death.

Question 3.
• Buddhism • Hinduism • Islam • Judaism

Describe a time of the year that is important for members in **one** of the above world religions. In your answer you should explain why that time of year is important for followers today.

Question 4.
"The world is charged with the grandeur of God." – Gerard Manley Hopkins

Describe the key beliefs about God held by believers in **one** of the major world religions that you have studied. In your answer you should outline how the beliefs about God influence the way of life of followers of the world religion.

Question 5.
Ritual can help people to express their faith.
Discuss the importance of ritual for members of **one** of the following major world religions:
• Buddhism • Christianity • Hinduism • Islam • Judaism

Question 6.
Outline the work being done by **one** community of faith to promote justice. In your answer you should describe the religious moral vision on which this work is based.

PHOTO CREDITS

For permission to reproduce photos, the author and publisher gratefully acknowledge the following:

100 © Reuters; 103B © Topfoto; 103T © Corbis/Carmen Redondo; 104 © Lonely Planet Images/Richard Cummins.

The author and publisher have made every effort to trace all copyright holders, but if any has been inadvertently overlooked we would be pleased to make the necessary arrangements as the first opportunity.